Copyright © 2021 Hillsong International Ltd atf Hillsong International

Version 5

First edition was published 2007
Second edition 2009
Third edition 2014
Fourth edition 2018
Fifth edition 2019

All rights reserved. No part of this book may be reproduced in any form by any mechanical or electronic means including information storage or retrieval systems, without permission in writing from the publisher.

While the manual is consistent with the values of Hillsong, the program and manual are suitable for use within any value or faith-based system. The purpose of this community development program is to promote a holistic, humanitarian and strengths-based approach to life.

Enquiries should be addressed to the publishers.

Hillsong Music & Resources
PO Box 1195, Castle Hill NSW 1765, Australia

T: +61 2 8853 5300
F: +61 2 8846 4625
E: resources@hillsong.com

WARNING:

The ShineWOMEN Facilitator Handbook and ShineWOMEN Journals are provided to help facilitate the running of the ShineWOMEN program. Although the content of the program is copyright protected it does NOT constitute, or contain legal, medical or other advice. Use of this handbook and running the program is entirely at your own risk.

Before running this program, you should obtain your own legal, insurance and other professional advice in the State, Territory or Country in which you intend to run the program.

SHINEWOMEN FACILITATOR HANDBOOK

ACKNOWLEDGEMENTS SIX
INTRODUCTION SEVEN
SHINEWOMEN OVERVIEW EIGHT
PROGRAM INFORMATION ELEVEN
SESSION OUTCOMES THIRTY-FIVE
SESSION PLANS THIRTY-NINE
FOUNDATIONAL CONCEPT 1 – WORTH FORTY-THREE
SESSION ONE I AM VALUABLE FIFTY-ONE
SESSION TWO I AM ONE-OF-A-KIND SIXTY-ONE
SESSION THREE I AM WONDERFULLY MADE SEVENTY-ONE
FOUNDATIONAL CONCEPT 2 – STRENGTH EIGHTY-THREE
SESSION FOUR I HAVE THE POWER OF CHOICE EIGHTY-NINE
SESSION FIVE MY DECISIONS DETERMINE MY DESTINATION ONE HUNDRED AND FIVE
SESSION SIX I HAVE RESILIENCE ONE HUNDRED AND SEVENTEEN
FOUNDATIONAL CONCEPT 3 – PURPOSE ONE HUNDRED AND TWENTY-FIVE
SESSION SEVEN MY POTENTIAL IS LIMITLESS ONE HUNDRED AND THIRTY-ONE
SESSION EIGHT MY LIFE HAS PURPOSE ONE HUNDRED AND FORTY-ONE
SESSION NINE SHINE! ONE HUNDRED AND FIFTY-FIVE
APPENDICES ONE HUNDRED AND SIXTY

acknowledgements.

We would like to acknowledge and thank the following contributors:

DR NANDILLA SPRY DBA, MSD, BA, CERT IV TAE

RENEE YAM M. SEXUAL HEALTH, PGDIPSOCHLTH, CERT IV TAA, B. EC.

CELINA MINA M. ED. (INT. ED.), B. ED., B. ARTS, A. MUS. A.

SARAH MCMAHON BA (PSYCH), PG DIP (PSYCH), PG DIP (PSYCH PR) ASSOC MAPS

LYDIA JADE TURNER BA (PSYCH) PG DIP (PSYCH) ASSOC MAPS

JO WHITE R.N. CERT IV, AOD, CERT IV TAA

LESLEY SHIELDS CERT IV IN SOCIAL WELFARE, CERT III IN COUNSELLING

WE WOULD LIKE TO THANK **VERA COLEMAN** FOR MAKING IT POSSIBLE TO START THIS JOURNEY IN 1997. THE ULTIMATE TEST OF AN IDEA IS WHETHER IT OUTLIVES US. CHANGING THE WORLD IS A COLLABORATIVE EFFORT. HER COMMITMENT CREATED MANY OPPORTUNITIES FOR WOMEN AND GIRLS ALL OVER THE WORLD TO FLOURISH.

introduction.

ShineWOMEN is about equipping women with the knowledge and skills to discover who they are and the person they want to become. This program encourages participants to find the strength and courage within them to make healthy choices and live to their full potential. The program is not aimed at stereotyping what women should be like or how they should behave, but using a holistic approach, it reinforces that every woman is different and has different strengths, qualities and skills. Sharing knowledge to open conversations about the uniqueness of each person is a direct affront to dominant ideas of what makes one beautiful. These ideas subjugate women and contribute to non-agentive positions by which women grade their worth and value.

The ShineWOMEN program provides the opportunity to create communities of concern and also hopes to offer women new agentive positions to co-construct stories of identity in which they discover a new language to speak about what they value and treasure in their lives, and to state their hopes and preferences. Many women in our communities do not know or believe they are valuable and unique individuals. Most struggle with this concept due to the pressures of daily life and responsibility. ShineWOMEN therefore aims to address common issues such as poor self-acceptance, shame, condemnation, low confidence as a result of fear and other causes, providing skills to navigate and overcome challenges through activities in a group environment. The program emphasises that to value others, we need to first value ourselves. Understanding what is valuable to a person will assist in their decision-making and relationship skills. Additionally, this welfare-based program addresses outcomes from key learning areas that apply to many other courses supporting women's personal development. The structure of ShineWOMEN enables facilitators to differentiate the content based on the individual learning needs of the participating women and can also be modified for individual learning plans.

The methodologies used include active participation and discussion forums. Therefore, such methods have been found to assist with social confidence, how to work with peers in a team or towards a goal, how to speak up for themselves and to learn how to express emotions in a healthy manner.

The program demonstrates that:
- Each individual can make a unique contribution to the world
- Anger and emotions can be released in a healthy way
- To gain respect we need to first respect others
- Overcoming challenges and taking risks can grow a person's character
- Making informed choices can reduce the risk of negative consequences.

overview.

ShineWOMEN is a unique personal development and group mentoring tool that uses an inspirational, practical and experiential approach to learning. This program is founded upon the premise that every life counts and has intrinsic value, and fosters an awareness of this belief. As a result, women are equipped to become effective global citizens for the future.

aim.

For each woman to develop understanding of her own personal worth, strength and purpose and realise the potential within her to fulfil her desires.

objectives.

Equip women to:
Identify themselves as valuable with much to contribute
Build confidence, self-esteem and self-worth
Develop respect and boundaries in relationships
Understand they are able to have a positive influence in their world
Identify personal desires and strengths to motivate them to set and achieve personal goals

These message objectives are achieved through:

three foundational concepts: worth. strength. purpose.

i have WORTH!

'BODY AND SOUL, I AM WONDERFULLY MADE'

The focus for these sessions is for you to understand for yourself that you are valuable.
Your uniqueness is something to celebrate and you have been wonderfully made.

i have STRENGTH!

'CHOOSE LIFE'

These sessions explore the power of choice and the power that decisions have on shaping a person's future.
This is addressed through practical sessions about feelings, convictions, decision-making and problem-solving.

i have PURPOSE!

'I HAVE A HOPE AND A FUTURE'

Purpose is examined through exploring personal hopes, dreams and desires.
Goal setting, group discussions on potential talents and practical activities, are used to equip
and build confidence to live out a purpose-filled, adventurous life.

SHINEWOMEN

PI

program information.

key outcomes.

Women have achieved learning and motivational outcomes that form the foundation of the ultimate goal – a greater level of understanding about their own personal worth, strength and purpose.

These include:
- Developed holistic personal and problem-solving skills
- Improved confidence and understanding of value
- Enhanced social support networks
- Greater understanding in relation to gifts and talents
- Greater awareness of community contribution and participation

strengths-based approach.

ShineWOMEN focuses on addressing the strengths and skills the participants possess rather than their weaknesses or deficits. All people have strengths but many are unrecognised and unused by the individual. The strengths-based approach inspires participants to grow and change by using their strengths as a personal resource. As people become engaged through experiential and interactive activities, participants can begin to discover their inner strength, skills, personal identity and qualities.

ShineWOMEN encourages participants to become the expert within their own life. They are the ones who can tap into their own potential and discover their personal identity and worth. Ultimately, the process of discovering and understanding 'the self' always comes from within the participant's own perspective. The facilitator is there to draw out the best from each participant and to be a guide in the process.

experiential learning.

ShineWOMEN applies experiential learning to purposefully engage participants through direct experience and focused reflection in order to increase knowledge, develop problem-solving skills and clarify concepts. Practical sessions are designed to create a non-confronting environment for women that helps remove communication barriers and assists in building rapport in the relationships between participants and facilitators.

The facilitators' role is to organise and facilitate experiences that lead to genuine learning. Our hope is that such learning will create long-lasting and meaningful memories for each participant. This often requires the group to partake in preparatory and reflective exercises.

METHODS TO FACILITATE LEARNING INCLUDE:

VISUAL – videos, charts, whiteboards, notes
AUDITORY – discussions, interviews, music, personal stories, short teaching sessions, audios
KINAESTHETIC – role plays, physical activity, small group work, whole group work

Interaction and contribution by participants promotes understanding and empowers people to move forward, using skills learnt within the group.

team building.

There are many different roles and responsibilities in implementing the ShineWOMEN program, so we advise to build a team for maximum impact and success. For example, in a class of 15 participants, there could be one facilitator and one or two co-facilitators depending on what the session requires.

TEAM PHILOSOPHY

ShineWOMEN encourages facilitators to create a unique neutral environment which can reduce any feeling of an 'us and them' culture. In using the analogy of a train ride, all the participants join together to travel the journey. This is why the program is best facilitated with a strong team who are supportive, great listeners and skilled at facilitating. Ultimately, it's the team carrying the message within ShineWOMEN.

ESTABLISHING A TEAM

It's important to take the time to build a good team with people you have met personally, who you believe are reliable and have possibly built relationship with. You and the organisation you represent are accountable for the behaviour and actions of your team. It is important to properly screen the applicants even though you might know them well. Follow your organisation's procedures with regard to the recruitment and involvement of the team, volunteers and guest presenters.

If there is no procedure, establish one with an application form and consider the applicant in the following areas:
- Related qualifications and/or experience
- Suitability to work with participants and issues they face
- Length of time you have known them
- References: 2 referees (log the responses on the form)
- Duration of time the applicant can commit to involvement is a minimum of 12 months.

Your team members or co-facilitators are a valuable asset to the group. It is important to care for and build into each individual team member, becoming aware of their limitations and be able to nurture their particular gifts and skills. Building and investing into your team contributes to making ShineWOMEN more effective and promotes its success in the community.

TEAM ROLES

Outlined below are team roles that can be established within the program.

FACILITATOR: The facilitator is the one who leads each session and maintains the structure and fluidity of each session.

CO-FACILITATOR: The co-facilitator comes alongside the facilitator and can be trained to eventually run the sessions.

PRESENTERS: Presenters are guests who may be invited to speak or share their story on a particular session topic. This could be for 10 minutes or up to a maximum of 30 minutes but it is advised to not go for the length of the whole session.

SET-UP: This is a coordinator role, which ensures that the room and any props or materials required are ready for the session. Set-up includes: Room set-up, Preparation of refreshments, Resources for the day – pens, paper, items for activities, photocopies.

SUPPORT PERSON: ShineWOMEN is NOT a counselling session. The support person is there as a friend and to 'come alongside' participants during the sessions only. The scope of team roles is not limited to the above, as roles can expand and grow depending on your own organisational structure and local setting. Other suggestions can include: Advertising the program in your community, Seeking sponsorship and funding, Pathway options in your organisation, Partnering with other organisations and community development.

Note: The ShineWOMEN program values excellence; as a team, decide to place excellence on everything that is being carried out. This also demonstrates the value that is placed on the individual.

outworking a session.

BRIEF
Allow time to brief your team on the plan for the session. Communication is vital for the team to operate together, so make sure each team member knows what is required of them and that all tasks are delegated. People are empowered to contribute when given responsibility. Participants can tell if a team is not operating cohesively.

PREPARE
ShineWOMEN takes time, organisation and thought. The effort that is made for the participants signifies the value that is placed on them. Every aspect of group preparation creates an atmosphere of value.

It is a good idea to organise the items and resources needed for the session in advance and have a checklist so that the team is not running around moments before the program is due to start. Being organised and mentally prepared allows the facilitator to remain calm and 'present' with the group.

session facilitation and implementation.

When we are in the group, from start to finish, be 'present'. Give 100% attention and energy to the group and the participants. Decide on excellence, as everything we do speaks and demonstrates the value we place on each individual.

DEBRIEF
It is important for facilitators and the team to debrief with each other after each session. This allows the team to reflect back and evaluate the session and prepare for the following week. Debriefing encourages personal reflection, allowing the opportunity to identify any triggers that may be present within themselves that may create an issue in facilitating the course the following week.

FOLLOW UP
Allow time to follow up with the participants in the group, particularly if they are going through a difficult time. If possible, connect them into established pathways such as community services, counselling and/or support groups.

getting started.

ShineWOMEN is best implemented when it is well supported and under the leadership of your local organisation.

VENUE

Ensure the venue is 'environmentally friendly' and easy to access. This includes:
- Space for all the participants to sit comfortably
- Teaching aids available
- Low noise
- Safe – windows, doors, clean and uncluttered hazard-free room
- Accessibility after hours.

SET-UP

One of the keys to demonstrating value to the participants is doing everything with excellence. This may be emphasised through actions, speech and personal attitudes. During set-up, facilitators are encouraged to take time in preparing the room and to also be creative!

The presentation of the room can create a responsive, warm, friendly and open atmosphere. This is probably the first thing the participants will encounter. Setting up the room differently to regular classes can create anticipation. It also shows that you believe the students are worth the effort of arriving early and setting up the room nicely. It adds another layer that communicates value.

Changing the room for different sessions and concepts can increase learning capacity.
Invite intrigue by covering props and having hidden surprises. This stirs emotions and lifts expectations.

Practical tips for set-up:
- Keep the set-up design simple and modern.
- Make sure the room is safe, uncluttered and comfortable.
- Take into account lighting, sound and positioning of furniture.

ATMOSPHERE
A ShineWOMEN group could best be described as feeling like the women are sitting in their living room, talking about current concerns they need to talk about whilst relaxing and having fun. There are a number of elements that impact on atmosphere:

SEATING
If possible, move all the chairs and tables into a square or circle so that everyone can see each other. Have the facilitators spread out around the circle so they are part of the group. Stay seated when you are speaking or presenting. Being on the same level as the group can reduce intimidation and make it easier to relate to the participants.

VISUAL
Basic items that can be used as props for a session can make a huge difference to the way the room looks. You can be as creative as you like, but it doesn't have to be too complicated. The session title on the board can stir up curiosity. Collages and posters with words or quotes on them are also excellent for participants who are visual learners.

MUSIC
During the first few weeks it is great to have music playing. The right music can create a fun atmosphere. It also takes away any awkward silences. Music with positive lyrics can also be a powerful message to help communicate the concepts you are trying to get across. You may choose to have music playing throughout the session or just during certain parts, such as the activities. Again, music can also be a distraction if it is too loud, so it is important to keep that in mind.

BUDGET
Be creative with the budget you have. Also see our tips on applying for funding.

shineWOMEN guidelines.

Establishing group guidelines is a way of setting boundaries within the group and reinforcing respect and value for one another. Guidelines are formed in partnership with the group as to what should be acceptable and not acceptable. It focuses on how to respect and value each other rather than establishing rules and regulations. Emphasise that the reason we use the agreement form is to build trust, and create safety in sharing their opinion or opening up to the group. This is also an opportunity to screen the women in case there are concerns of serious psychological problems, victims of trauma or abuse, mental health, learning difficulties and so forth. However, it is up to the organisation that has already identified the women to determine who is not suitable for group work. In this case, seeking a professional psychologist or counsellor might be an option.

CONFIDENTIALITY

The information discussed during the groups is usually of a personal nature and may not have been told to anyone else. It could be information about their fears, relationships, or the difficulties they encounter in their life. They are allowing themselves to become vulnerable to us on the basis that the information remains confidential. We endeavour to establish a professional relationship with participants, while at the same time partnering alongside them as they discover their unique identity and self-worth. However, the duty of confidentiality is not an absolute. There are certain times when we are required to override confidentiality.

For example:
- When required to by law – for example, court order, a major crime, mandatory reporting
- When it's in the 'public interest' – for example, a public health issue
- When the person is harming themself or others, or at risk of doing so
- When it is a part of a 'treatment'/'support' team, and then only what the participant consents to being revealed.

To maintain a professional code of ethics, group members need to be assured that generally, information they share within the group will be kept confidential amongst the group members and facilitators.

SUPPORT FOR PARTICIPANTS AND FACILITATORS

There are some sessions which can cause challenging personal issues to surface for the group participants. Counsellors or social workers should be available on site when the group is implemented in the case of matters arising for the participants, or for facilitators to debrief after a session when required.

pathways.

Pathways are simply about the next step after ShineWOMEN. Your pathway approach will be unique to your organisation. This gives you the opportunity to facilitate initiatives within your organisation relevant to the participants that you have connected with. Connection and relationship with the participants are formed throughout.

Whilst ShineWOMEN is complete in itself, follow-up steps through pathway ideas can be very beneficial. Some ideas may include social outings, justice projects helping others, activities, social groups and so forth. Pathway options can also include connecting women to community services such as:

- Counselling
- Nutrition/exercise programs
- Education
- Volunteer work
- Employment
- Women's centres
- Financial budgeting
- Health care
- Mentoring between women in business and women in charity and the non-profit sector.

getting started SUMMARY

MAKE SURE YOUR VENUE IS 'ENVIRONMENTALLY FRIENDLY'.

ENSURE THAT EVERYTHING YOU DO, INCLUDING ROOM SET-UP, PRESENTATION, ADVERTISING AND PROMOTION IS DONE WITH EXCELLENCE AND COMMUNICATES VALUE.

BUILD A STRONG TEAM AND ALLOCATE ROLES AND RESPONSIBILITIES TO EACH TEAM MEMBER.

ENSURE CONFIDENTIALITY AND TRUST IS DEVELOPED AND MAINTAINED WITHIN THE GROUP AND YOUR TEAM.

THINK ABOUT WHAT PATHWAYS YOU CAN CONNECT THE WOMEN TO AFTER COMPLETING SHINEWOMEN. WHAT ARE THEIR NEEDS AND WHAT IS OUT IN THE COMMUNITY FOR THEM?

facilitator information.

An important skill in running ShineWOMEN is facilitation. Facilitation is about leading a group toward a desired outcome and encouraging active participation from all members in the group. So unless the facilitators of this program are teachers, it is strongly encouraged that each group has at least one accredited facilitator and a facilitator-in-training. The accredited facilitator should have (or is working towards) accredited membership with the Institute of Group Leaders (www.igl.org.au). To be eligible for accredited membership you must:

- Complete a 30-hour group work training course (acceptable to the Institute)
- Facilitate at least 80 hours within the past three years
- Receive regular supervision for the group work facilitation
- Attend regular continuing education workshops.

Facilitation is about them, not you. Be yourself and don't be afraid to be genuine. Remember to be a positive role model. Some participants rarely have opportunities to connect with positive role models. The following summary is helpful to read before each session.

KEY CHARACTERISTICS OF GOOD FACILITATION

- Empathy
- Listening skills
- Confidence
- Maintaining a level of control so the outcome of the session is achieved
- Being able to create an environment that is harmonious
- Knowing your session content
- Achieving set outcomes
- Meeting the needs of both the facilitator and participant throughout each session
- Creating a safe environment

ESSENCE OF FACILITATION:
- Draw out ideas and input from the group
- Exude a friendly attitude
- Give clear direction
- Work in a team environment
- Make things easier so that the group achieves together
- Be diplomatic and non-judgmental
- Analyse situations and assess needs
- Have the ability to handle conflict and hostility
- Involve yourself, yet remain objective
- Have the ability to remember names and session processes
- Encourage contributions from participants
- Be empathetic and actively listen to each participant and team member.

CHARACTERISTICS THAT HINDER GOOD FACILITATION:
- Poor preparation
- Imposing personal values or views
- Being too directive or passive
- Assumptions about session knowledge
- Not being clear about the purpose of the group
- Low expectation of participants
- Talking all the time
- Spotlighting a shy participant
- Giving 'answers' vs the group learning from each other.

KNOW YOURSELF
- Understand yourself and others
- Recognise your strengths and the areas where you can improve
- Keep a sense of humour.

THE PROCESS AND ACTIVITIES FACILITATORS USE NEED TO:
- Be consistent with the core concepts
- Create opportunities for people to hear each other's experiences i.e. seat people in a circle
- Achieve session outcomes
- Build relationship with participants.

FACILITATORS ARE:
- Relational
- Analysers
- Supporters
- Purposeful

FACILITATORS DO NOT:
- Counsel or fix people
- Fulfil the role of friends, family or partners
- Become the experts.

effective communication.

Effective communication is essential for a balanced lifestyle. Participants and facilitators are simultaneously sending and receiving a variety of messages. A skilled facilitator will take advantage of body language as well as verbal communication in order to receive messages that the participants are expressing. Body language includes eye movements, facial expressions, head nods, posture, gestures, arm movements, leg positioning and physical positioning.

When communicating within the group be aware not to use 'jargon', as it may cause separation or barriers for those who don't understand the words. There may be times when it is appropriate but only if you are sure it fits within the discussion.

There are several positive ways to enhance communication between the facilitator and participant. The following briefly highlights some techniques to improve our ability to communicate with participants.

BODY LANGUAGE:

Non-verbal cues or body language play a key role in the communication process. Observing how people are saying what they are saying can tell you much more about the content of the message, than the words themselves. Our facial expressions, body movements, posture, position and gestures all play a critical role when we communicate with others.

EYE CONTACT:
AVOID EXTREMES – don't zero in and lock eyes with any one person for an extended period of time; on the other hand, don't sweep your eyes too fast over the group.

BE NATURAL – don't establish a set pattern of eye contact (for example, the 'windshield wiper' approach to eye contact).

VOICE AND LANGUAGE:
- Know what you are going to say before you say it
- Be positive, friendly and straightforward
- Refrain from reading your notes or written materials as much as possible
- When presenting or facilitating discussions, remain enthusiastic
- Make sure you can be heard comfortably by listeners
- Watch your pace and articulation
- Rehearse your presentation beforehand, read it aloud, and get feedback if possible
- Choose your words carefully (say what you mean!)
- Have a glass of water (or a sour lemon drop) handy to counter a dry throat or a persistent 'tickle'.

tips on group dynamics.

BE A ROLE MODEL
Our behaviour is a model to participants at all times. Model a sensitive, patient and tolerant approach to the issues that are presented in the group. Listen attentively when participants share experiences, or when emotions are being expressed. Never make light of people's experiences or discount their feelings. However, balance the needs of individuals with the needs of the group as a whole. Also try to explain issues and to respond in ways that maintain participants' intrinsic worth, without appearing strongly biased concerning the subject matter.

DON'T KNOW EVERYTHING
Although you may possess extensive knowledge pertaining to the subject matter, periodically you may get a question that you are unable to answer. Don't hesitate to admit that you don't know the answer but advise the group that you will find out and follow up with them.

ENCOURAGE PARTICIPANTS

Encourage participation and the sharing of ideas, while maintaining the focus of the discussion. Some participants will have never discussed the subject material in a formal context before. Sharing experiences can help the whole group to gain a better understanding. Differences in opinion and approach are normal. Allow differences of opinion to be expressed. Create an atmosphere in which participants do not feel judged because of their beliefs.

Don't get into debates or try to 'win' arguments with participants. We all have the right to our own opinion. At the same time, be aware of those participants who are quieter than others and encourage them to join the discussions.

KNOW YOUR PARTICIPANTS

This course has specific learning or performance objectives. Knowing your group can help you:
- Stay focused and on track
- Create opportunities for participants to resolve issues that are important for them
- Anticipate discomfort or particular problems
- Be prepared for strong feelings on certain issues
- Obtain as much information as possible about the group prior to implementing the message.
- Background on their familiarity with the subject material, experience, and current related issues can be helpful.

AWKWARD SITUATIONS

Periodically, challenging situations will arise when facilitating the course. Experienced facilitators will have developed 'tried and proven' techniques for handling and responding to many of these; however, for the new facilitator, challenges can be somewhat intimidating. What if the group won't respond? What if one participant adamantly disagrees with the rest of the group? What if everyone is talking at once? These situations periodically occur throughout any group. Some suggested techniques for handling them are covered in the following paragraphs.

TOO QUIET
Tactfully draw the participant out, but don't force them too early in the course. Some participants need more time to relax and feel comfortable. Don't assume that they don't have anything to contribute; it may mean that they just need to be encouraged. It may help if this participant is not seated next to a talkative individual. If they appear receptive, ask for their thoughts on the topic under discussion – especially when you know she has experience or ideas on the topic. Another suggestion could be to ask the young person to help pack up chairs with you and your team at the end of the session. You can use this opportunity to build rapport and encourage them.

PRIVATE CONVERSATIONS IN THE GROUP
Private conversations may be an indication of keen interest in the subject or of participants becoming distracted on other matters. Give gentle reminders of what was covered in the group guidelines. This will usually draw their attention back to the group without 'turning-off' participants.

TALKATIVE
It helps to distinguish between a very knowledgeable participant who is making a relevant contribution and the participant who is dominating and distracting the group. However, both need to be validated and encouraged to feel valued. We should not 'close down' a person but rather redirect their comments at perhaps a breathing space or thought interval – jump in and validate them by saying 'That's right, thank you' or 'That's where we were going' and then continue with your plan.

GROUP CONFLICT
It is never permissible for group members to be disrespectful or abusive toward one another. If you witness participants treating others in ways that may be harmful or hurtful, you must step in to help redirect the atmosphere. One way of addressing the issue is to reiterate the group guidelines established at the beginning of the course – for example, when one person is talking everyone should listen, even if they do not agree on what is being said. Allow every person to have an opportunity to present their opinion.

LACK OF GROUP ENERGY
When a group loses dynamics, becomes predictable or stale, there are no limits to the creative actions you can take to breathe some life into a group – using humour, spontaneous actions, exercise, role-playing – almost anything to get energy flowing.

EMOTIONALLY DISTRESSED PARTICIPANT
If you are noticing a participant who is visibly withdrawn, upset or emotional, approach them quietly and ask them if they are ok. Use discernment and don't make it obvious to the whole group. If a participant is displaying behaviour that is separate to the group behaviour or was different to previous sessions, ask them a few questions to see if everything is ok for them and encourage them to take deep breaths, slow their breathing down, drink some water and ask if they would like to see a social/welfare worker or counsellor.

SCAPEGOATING
Facilitators are to be conscious that scapegoating at this age is quite common. The word scapegoat has multiple meanings but primarily is when an individual knowingly allows oneself to be blamed in order to maintain the group's homogeneity. However, that individual may be an unwilling participant as it is common for the group to put down a participant in order to maintain the group's cohesion. Scapegoating can be addressed through team building activities, guest speakers and group discussions.

PARTICIPANT BEHAVIOUR
As a facilitator, be aware of inappropriate behaviour. This could include late arrivals, negativity, not participating or being argumentative. Participants need to be informed that it is inappropriate to attend the group if they are under the influence of drugs or alcohol. This should not be seen as a failure in having a successful group, but a solution in ensuring that the remainder of the group succeeds in achieving their goal. If a situation was to arise, do not undertake this on your own; rather, it's best to discuss with the supervisor or co-facilitator and then speak with the participant involved.

CLOSURE

When bringing the group towards closure, advice on other groups or support groups can be suggested if participants feel that they would like to continue to focus on their goals.

At the time of closure, recognition of people's achievement in completing the program can be made by presenting them with a Certificate of Achievement. This acknowledges the work and contribution of each person, gives a sense of completion and can be used as a tool, which may be included in resumes. See Appendix I for a sample of the certificate.

Thank each participant for their co-operation and willingness in working together as a team and encourage them in their future endeavours and successes.

shineWOMEN facilitator requirements and expectations.

MINIMUM REQUIREMENTS

- Commitment to facilitating ShineWOMEN as per the organisation's request.
- Ensure an appropriate amount of time for preparation before a session.
- Work in collaboration with co-facilitators.
- Represent your organisation and the ShineWOMEN message in a professional manner. This includes both appropriate behaviour and clothing.
- Commit to every group with excellence being of the highest quality possible.

LIMITATIONS

NEVER FORCE A PARTICIPANT TO DO SOMETHING THEY ARE NOT COMFORTABLE DOING.

For example, if you make a shy person answer a question in front of the group, chances are they will shut down for the rest of the program.

facilitator INFORMATION SUMMARY

BE YOURSELF.

WE ARE NOT HERE TO BE THE EXPERT OR PROFESSIONAL. WE ARE HERE TO CREATE AN ENVIRONMENT WHERE THE WOMEN CAN ENCOUNTER THE TRUTH OF WHO THEY ARE.

BE CREATIVE.

USE EVERYTHING TO REINFORCE THE CONCEPTS AND EACH PARTICIPANT'S VALUE.

BE PURPOSEFUL IN EVERYTHING YOU DO.

BE EXCELLENT. BE THE BEST YOU CAN BE. THE STANDARD WE DO THINGS DIRECTLY REFLECTS THE VALUE OF THE PARTICIPANT.

BE UNCONDITIONAL IN LOVE AND ACCEPTANCE OF THE PARTICIPANTS.

BUILD AN AWESOME TEAM.

KEEP THE ELEMENT OF SURPRISE.

have fun and enjoy the experience!

fundraising.

In the current fundraising environment of fewer dollars and more not-for-profit (NFP) organisations, we can't afford to waste our time and resources. Here are some suggestions of the type of information to provide for more successful fundraising:

BE CLEAR ABOUT:
- Who you are and what you do
- Who will benefit from these activities or services
- The community need you are addressing
- Your expected outcomes
- How your mission addresses that need
- Your measures of success
- The precise activities or services for which you are seeking support
- The type and amount of resources you need to achieve your desired result.

INVEST IN PROSPECT RESEARCH

Once you are clear about your needs, shift your focus to the needs of your potential donors. Learn their history and their unique interests. Learn their guidelines, policies and grant-making procedures. Learn their funding patterns, including the specific types of grants and the dollar amounts. The more information you gather the more likely it is that you will be able to find a realistic match.

CREATE VALUE

Not-for-profit organisations exist to make a difference. But in order to attract funding, you must be able to answer two key questions:
- How will your request help the donor meet their philanthropic goals?
- In what specific ways will the donor benefit from contributing to your organisation?
- If you can develop a compelling statement describing how they will benefit from your outcomes, you have probably found a good match.

In addition, demonstrate that you are a mission-focused and a results-oriented organisation by:
- Presenting a well-developed plan for implementing and evaluating your activities
- Providing evidence of your competence and capacity to deliver, documenting that you will be able to sustain your proposed activities.

PLEASE NOTE: As previously detailed, you will need to seek independent legal advice to ensure you are legally compliant for fundraising in your jurisdiction.

BUILD COMMUNITY PARTNERSHIPS

Foundation and corporate funders receive many more requests than they are able to fund. They are keenly aware of the duplication that is prevalent in the non-profit sector and the large number of non-profits requesting funds to address related issues.

- Corporations and foundations are more likely to fund requests (and to give higher amounts) if the work plan demonstrates a true partnership among several organisations. Working through territory and other issues is difficult, but it is worth the effort.
- All of us spend a great deal of time raising money from corporations and foundations. Investing time and resources in researching the most likely prospects increases the chances for success. Focusing on the benefits that organisations will gain from supporting you will increase your chances even more.

FUNDING AND SPONSORSHIP

Internet – search websites such as *communitybuilders.nsw.gov.au* and *philanthropy.org.au* as well as the classified section of major newspapers. Requests for tenders may also be included in the business section or in other areas of the paper.

- Local government bodies
- Local council
- Professionals in your community
- In-kind donations
- Sponsorship on items used for supplies
- An organisation may want to 'sponsor-a-woman' for the duration of the message.

PREPARE YOUR PROPOSAL

- **BACKGROUND** – Who are you? What does your organisation do? Be brief and to the point.
- **NEED** – What is the need? Provide statistics – demonstrate that you know your community and that you have done your homework.
- **GOAL OR PURPOSE** – State your desired outcomes, what do you want to achieve? Structure and Management: How would the message be structured and managed?
- **TIMEFRAME** - When would it start/finish?
- **SUMMARY BUDGET** - Ballpark figures – capital needed, overheads, income. This can be done in a simple table.

Promotion may be achieved through networking. Often there are people in your network who could support your work in Shine. Source people who have fundraising or submission writing experience.

NOTE: This Facilitator Guide and accompanying Journals are provided to help facilitate the running of the Shine program. Although the content of the program is copyright protected it does NOT constitute, or contain legal, medical or other advice. Use of this handbook and running the program, is entirely at your own risk.

SHINEWOMEN

session outcomes.

Each session allows the women to participate in an experiential and interactive activity and have the opportunity to socially interact and connect with participants and facilitators.

worth.

SESSION 1: I AM VALUABLE
By the end of this session, each woman will be able to:
Gain an understanding of the concept of value
Identify what she personally values and why
Develop an awareness of personal value

SESSION 2: I AM ONE-OF-A-KIND
By the end of this session, each woman will be able to:
Recognise the value of being one-of-a-kind
Distinguish the difference between uniqueness and comparison

SESSION 3: I AM WONDERFULLY MADE
By the end of this session, each woman will be able to:
Have an understanding of the Worth concept
Identify ways to value herself

strength.

SESSION 4: I HAVE THE POWER OF CHOICE
By the end of this session, each woman will be able to:
Explore and understand that she is born with feelings
Demonstrate skills required to enhance the power of choice

SESSION 5: MY DECISIONS DETERMINE MY DESTINATION
By the end of this session, each woman will be able to:
Apply and practise decision-making and problem-solving skills
Recognise the value of respect and convictions

SESSION 6: I HAVE RESILIENCE
By the end of this session, each woman will be able to:
Recognise the value of developing resilience

purpose.
SESSION 7: MY POTENTIAL IS LIMITLESS
By the end of this session, each woman will be able to:
Recognise the value of a positive environment for her potential to grow
Identify ways to build her confidence

SESSION 8: MY LIFE HAS PURPOSE
By the end of this session, each woman will be able to:
Identify personal desires
Develop an understanding that she has something to contribute

shine.
SESSION 9: SHINE!
By the end of this session, each woman will be able to:
Describe what she has learnt

It is important to reinforce the foundational concepts throughout the sessions, to reveal the truth that the life of every individual woman counts and that she has intrinsic value.

SHINEWOMEN

SP
session plans.

Session Plans.

ShineWOMEN is designed to be presented in 7 to 9, 60 to 90 minute weekly sessions. This can be adapted to other formats if necessary. The format is designed to enable the sessions to be adapted to other timeframes with ease.

The sessions are flexible in delivery, order and style of presentation; however, we recommend maintaining the order where possible. The key is to creatively express the specific concept each week and to create an environment where the participants experience and have understanding about the concepts presented.

Introduce the foundational concept at the beginning of each session, reinforcing it throughout and concluding each session with a brief overview of the concept by asking questions or giving the women an opportunity to ask questions.

FOUNDATIONAL CONCEPT
Everything we say and all the activities we do should relate to the three foundational concepts: Worth, Strength and Purpose.

OUTCOMES
Each session has its own identified outcomes. Teamwork activities are incorporated into each session to build trust, a sense of belonging, interpersonal skills, collaboration and the opportunity to learn and grow from each other.

Session Plans.
The following are the ingredients of the actual sessions:

ICEBREAKER
Each session begins with an icebreaker ideally relevant to the concept. You can investigate the web for icebreakers and energisers or see the alternative icebreakers in Appendix A. Icebreakers capture the attention of the participants. Their purpose is to 'break the ice' through a fun activity at the start of the session so the women are ready to receive, engage and get involved in the rest of the session.

POWER FOCUS
This is used to open up and introduce the concept and topic. It's designed to be specific and sharp and can include definitions, brainstorming or illustrations.

LAYING THE FOUNDATION
This is where the session outcomes are explained and the concept and topic are launched through illustrations, group discussions and demonstrations. Recommended teaching time is a maximum of 10 minutes.

PRESENTATION
This is the primary practical activity to achieve the outcomes. It is a chance for the participants to understand and explore the concept presented. Professionals can also be organised to present on the topic. Recommended time is 30 minutes.

GROUP DISCUSSION AND WRAP-UP
Get the participants to break up into small groups for the last 5 – 10 minutes of every session. Where possible, the participants should stay in the same small group with the same facilitator for the entire message. Small groups are a great opportunity for the team to connect with the women. This is the assessment component to establish if outcomes were achieved. Ask the participants questions that will help to summarise, recap and wrap up the session. Encourage the groups to share what they have learnt.

NOTE TO FACILITATOR
The discussion topics are flexible in delivery. As the facilitator, it is vital you understand your group and the best way to deliver the topics in order to engage the group and draw them into the discussion. Reading straight from the facilitator handbook to your group is not recommended. Use your own creativity and initiative to bring each topic to life, making it relatable to your target audience.

SHINE FACTOR
This is the special extra we give each woman to communicate the message of value. These gifts should relate to the session. Quotes or a key quote from the session allows the women to take something positive home with them. It creates a positive memory and enhances learning. It's up to you how creative you can be. Examples of ideas are included in each session plan.

'BODY AND SOUL, I AM WONDERFULLY MADE'

worth.

SESSION ONE I AM VALUABLE
SESSION TWO I AM ONE-OF-A-KIND
SESSION THREE I AM WONDERFULLY MADE

BASIS. 'BODY AND SOUL, I AM WONDERFULLY MADE.'

Introduction.

I have worth! This needs to mean more than just a nice statement – it is an encounter and an unveiling of what worth actually means.

'We have worth and will always have worth!'

To understand this concept, it means that it doesn't take status, reputation, honour, education, material richness, the latest fashions in our wardrobe and so forth to determine the worth inside of us. Even when everything else is stripped away from us, we have worth and will always have worth! We have it even now!

The concept of worth addresses and encourages self-acceptance, self-appreciation and self-love. It challenges the need to conform and to compare and encourages the discovery of how our worth impacts our unique identity.

The Worth concept explores:

i have worth! i am valuable! i am one-of-a-kind!
i am wonderfully made!

i am VALUABLE

We are not rubbish and we are not a mistake.

Our value has nothing to do with what we think or what people say about us. Our value is not attached to our performance. It is not based on our circumstances, family background, religion or socio-economic status.

Our value is linked to our very being – it is intrinsic. Value cannot be earned, regardless of what circumstances we find ourselves in; we all qualify for value and worth.

When something is valuable, it is precious and one-of-a-kind; a treasure…it has worth.

Each of us is set apart as unique; there is no one else like us! We are born one-of-a-kind, custom-built and a masterpiece!

UNIQUE

| *yoo*-neek |

A one-off, original, exceptional, rare, unequalled, extraordinary, incomparable, matchless, individual.

We are all different! This is something to celebrate.

DIFFERENT

| dif-er-*uh* nt |

Not the same, unlike, of other nature, form or quality.

FORTY-FIVE WORTH

i am ONE-OF-A-KIND

Each of us has a one-of-a-kind personality. The way we love is one-of-a-kind. Our personal style and creativity is one-of-a-kind. How we communicate is different. How we write or give expression to something is unique. If a group of people were to write about the same topic, not one paper would be written the same. That is because our personal expression of life is unique and one-of-a-kind.

i am WONDERFULLY FULLY *made.*

There are many facets and details of who we are. Every part of us has a purpose and a function. Our mind, body, emotions, personality, character, passions and dreams are all intricate parts of us. There are many characteristics that contribute to our individuality; our strengths, talents, laughter and smile have all been uniquely designed just for us. No one else is exactly the same. We have been designed just the way we are for a reason and a purpose. When we love something, we value it. Anything we love and adore, we treat with value. When we love ourselves, we are valuing ourselves.

note to facilitator.

We use the face as an illustration because the face is one of the first things people notice about others. We can tell a lot about a person through their face. Faces are personal, intimate and delicate. The worth activities engage women in a personal and intimate way and encourages them to embrace their natural one-of-a-kind beauty.

- These activities are not the focus for the sessions, but rather messages used to complement and accelerate the participants' learning of the Worth concept. They enable you to create a move into an organic practical experience in the classroom based on the school, girls, teachers, culture and environment. We are after the EXPERIENCE and the SKILL

- The activities are non-confrontational, tactile ways to engage and connect participants with each other and the facilitators; building relationship and rapport, creating trust, and openness, which is required for the Strength and Purpose sessions to be effective.

- All activities are designed to reinforce the foundational concept that each participant has value. Any activities undertaken within the Worth sessions should reinforce this concept.

"We have worth and will always have worth!"

'BODY AND SOUL, I AM WONDERFULLY MADE'

1

worth.

SESSION ONE | I AM VALUABLE

MATERIAL REQUIRED: Money note, 'I am valuable' handouts (see Appendix B), name badges, jewels x 2, brown paper bag, beautiful box for jewel, coloured permanent markers, big piece of paper, whiteboard markers, whiteboard **HAND MASSAGE MATERIALS:** Paper towels, raw sugar and oil (baby oil or olive oil), exfoliation product or hand cream, bowls (for sugar and oil)
Please see recommended layout below.

ACTIVITY	DETAILS	NOTES/MATERIALS
Introduction (15 mins)	Introduce the team. Explain the message and the outcomes. Ask the women to introduce themselves and explain what they are expecting from Shine. Establish group guidelines.	Come up with some group guidelines that can be displayed on the whiteboard.
Icebreaker (5 mins)	Illustration: Train Journey	
Power Focus (5 mins)	'I AM VALUABLE'	
Laying The Foundation (15 mins)	Group Discussion: You are valuable Demonstration: Local currency note Illustration: Jewel in paper bag vs. jewel in beautiful box.	RESOURCES: money note, 2 x jewels, paper bag, beautiful box, big piece of paper, coloured permanent markers.
Presentation (45 mins)	GROUP DISCUSSION: How do hands relate to value? Caring for our hands Group Activity: Hand massage	RESOURCES: oil, raw sugar, bowls or hand cream, handouts, whiteboard markers, whiteboard.
Group Discussion and Wrap-up (5 mins)	Q. What have you learnt about your own value today? Q. What can you do to show someone in your life that they are valuable? Reinforce the Worth concept 'I AM VALUABLE'.	
Shine Factor	As you give out the gifts, encourage each women	Gifts

outcomes.

By the end of this session, each women will be able to:

GAIN AN UNDERSTANDING OF THE CONCEPT OF VALUE
IDENTIFY WHAT SHE PERSONALLY VALUES AND WHY
DEVELOP AN AWARENESS OF PERSONAL VALUE

introduction.
Welcome the group.
The facilitator allows the team to introduce themselves and share why they are on the team and what they have learnt about Shine. Explain the message and the outcomes to the group. Encourage the women to introduce themselves to the group and explain what they are expecting from the message. Establish group guidelines.

icebreaker.
ILLUSTRATION: TRAIN JOURNEY

Imagine you are going on a train. You are waiting at the station to get on a train. You are embarking on a new journey; going to a new destination. There might be some apprehension or nerves about this next step. You will be travelling past varied scenery and stopping at different stations. Make sure you don't get off the train until you have reached your destination. What distractions might break the journey for you? Discuss.

Keep your eye on the destination. Commit yourself to this journey of ShineWOMEN… the journey of discovering YOU and your value!

power focus.
I AM VALUABLE

There are no mistakes! Life is created with a purpose and a reason for existence. We have been born for a reason, a purpose. No one has been created by mistake.

Our value has nothing to do with what we think or what people say about us. Our value is not attached to our performance. It is not based on our circumstances, family background, religion or socio-economic status. Human value is not determined by what people say about us. It's not determined by whether we have failed more times than we have succeeded. Our value is not determined by whether we have finished school, have a job, a car, a boyfriend or are popular. Circumstances like whether we are sick or healthy, rich or poor do not determine our value.

Our value is linked to our very being – it is intrinsic. Value cannot be earned, regardless of what circumstances we find ourselves in, we all qualify for value and worth.

Explore the questions:

Am I accepted?

Do I matter?

Do you see me?

Do you hear me?

Does what I am saying matter to you?

Do you recognise me?

Do your eyes light up when I am around?

Every one of us has this need for acceptance. It's a universal need. You matter! What you have to say matters. You are worth being cared about, listened to and validated. You are recognised. You are important.

laying the foundation.

GROUP DISCUSSION: YOU ARE VALUABLE
Emphasise to the women that living a life of value loves the woman within and gives her space to grow. This is a whole adventure to value.

DEMONSTRATION: LOCAL CURRENCY NOTE – FOR EXAMPLE, $5 OR $10
Here is a $10 note. What if I scrunched up this $10 note? What about if I stepped on it, crinkled it up and got it dirty? Would its value change? No, its value remains the same even if it isn't treated with care. No matter what happens to you, whether you have been treated well or you have been mistreated. You have not lost your value. We are valuable and we remain valuable.

ILLUSTRATION: JEWEL IN PAPER BAG VS. JEWEL IN BEAUTIFUL BOX
Hand out two jewels to two participants. One scrunched up in a paper bag, the other wrapped in a beautiful box. Ask them to both open up what they were given. Inside both is a jewel that carries exactly the same value. So no matter what's on the outside, intrinsically, we have this treasure inside that carries weight.

we are all
PRICELESS

presentation – value outworked.

GROUP DISCUSSION: HOW DO HANDS RELATE TO VALUE?

- Hands were never designed to cause harm to ourselves or to others. Hands are an extension of our gifts and talents into the world.
- Our hands are designed to serve us well and serve others well in love. A hurting humanity can end up having hands that hurt others, out it's not what our hands are meant to be doing.
- Hands are only one part of our amazing body. They are never insignificant and add to our worth as a human being.
- Every hand not only looks unique and is one-of-a-kind but every hand does unique things.

GROUP DISCUSSION: CARING FOR OUR HANDS

Explain interesting facts about hands (see Appendix C for handout sheet)

Brainstorm either in small groups or all together:

- What do we use our hands for?
- What are some things hands can do for people – helping and giving?

The demonstration below is only one example of our unique one-of-a-kind nature and individual form.

GROUP ACTIVITY: HAND MASSAGE

Use an exfoliating hand scrub or hand cream for this activity.

EXFOLIATING HAND SCRUB:

Make sure everyone has easy access to hand towels and locate where the nearest sink is.

Ask the women to get into pairs and explain the activity including what is in the scrub and the benefits of exfoliating regularly.

As an alternative to a product scrub, you can use olive or baby oil and raw sugar. Mix some oil with raw sugar and keep it a thick consistency. Give each woman a tablespoon full of the scrub. Ask the women to massage the scrub into their hands.

HAND MASSAGE: Ask the women to then pass around hand cream and give themselves a hand massage. Be aware of sensitive skin. See Appendix B for alternate activities.

discussion and wrap up.
Q. What can you do to show someone in your life that they are valuable?
Q. What have you learnt about your own value today?

ASSESS OUTCOMES
Reinforce the Worth concept. Affirm the group as a whole or to each individual by name – 'I am valuable.' This exercise is a powerful way to end the session.

shine factor.
IDEAS: Give gifts that relate to hands, such as hand or nail cream, exfoliating hand scrub or a henna tattoo.

note to facilitator.
Be creative with room set-up to create anticipation and atmosphere. This activity is a great opportunity for the facilitators to connect with the participants. Look out for women who may need extra care and encouragement.

'BODY AND SOUL, I AM WONDERFULLY MADE'

2

worth.

SESSION TWO | I AM ONE-OF-A-KIND

MATERIAL REQUIRED:

Shine Factor, name badges, whiteboard markers, whiteboard, picture of Mona Lisa and faces, big piece of blank paper. **FACE/HAIR MATERIALS:** Disposable wipes, small dishes, tissues and cotton wool balls, cleanser, moisturiser, sunscreen, hair bands, elastics, clips, bobby pins, mirrors, hair gel, mousse, oils, spray, combs, brushes.

Please see recommended layout below.

ACTIVITY	DETAILS	NOTES/MATERIALS
Icebreaker (10 mins)	Activity: Signature	RESOURCES: Whiteboard or hand out some paper.
Power Focus (10 mins)	'I AM ONE-OF-A-KIND.	
Laying The Foundation (10 mins)	Illustration: Mona Lisa Group Discussion: One-of-a-kind is beautiful	RESOURCES: picture of Mona Lisa, whiteboard markers, whiteboard.
Presentation (55 mins)	Activity: Staying fresh and highlighting your natural shine (face/hair)	RESOURCES: Hand out any relevant information and supplies to take the time to look after our face/hair.
Group Discussion and Wrap-up (5 mins)	Q. What have you learnt from today? Q. How would you describe worth in your own words? Reinforce Worth concept 'I AM ONE-OF-A-KIND.	
Shine Factor	As you give out the gifts, encourage each woman	Gifts

outcomes.

By the end of this session, each women will be able to:

RECOGNISE THE VALUE OF BEING ONE-OF-A-KIND

DISTINGUISH THE DIFFERENCE BETWEEN UNIQUENESS AND COMPARISON

icebreaker.

ACTIVITY: GIVE EXPRESSION TO OUR ONE-OF-A-KIND SIGNATURE

Put a piece of butcher's paper in the middle of the table. Ask the women to write their signature down. Emphasise the difference in handwriting and signatures. Once everyone has completed their signature, ask the women to stand back and look at all the drawings. No signature is the same.

Discuss with the women how they can give expression to their one-of-a-kind life. Ask the women to draw lines from their signature with the below questions for them to think about.

How does *my appearance* give expression to my one-of-a-kind life?

How does *my heritage and culture* give expression to my one-of-a-kind life?

How does *my personality and character* give expression to my one-of-a-kind life?

How does *my personal written signature* give expression to my one-of-a-kind life?

The participants may not be able to answer these questions easily, and that is okay. Use the questions as a discussion point to further unpack this concept of being one-of-a-kind.

Everyone has a different way of expressing their signature. Their signature is an expression of who they are; their personal style and their creativity. We are all responsible for bringing out the signature message in us. For alternative icebreakers see Appendix A.

SIGNATURE | sig-n*uh*-cher |

One-of-a-kind style, personality, culture, heart, passion and vocation.

one-of-a-kind is beautiful.

power focus.
'I AM ONE-OF-A-KIND.'

When something is one-of-a-kind, it is precious and valuable; it is a treasure…it has worth. Each of us is set apart as unique and there is no one like us! We are born one-of-a-kind, custom-built and a masterpiece!

UNIQUE
| *yoo*-neek |

A one-off, original, exceptional, rare, unequalled, extraordinary, incomparable, matchless, individual.

We are all different! This is something to celebrate.

DIFFERENT
| dif-er-*uh* nt |

Not the same, unlike, of other nature, form or quality.

One-of-a-kind is beautiful!
Conforming to what society and popular culture says is beautiful only steals from our uniqueness and creates sameness about every human being that is false and a thief to our identity. Also, sameness robs the world of the treasured one-of-a-kind way we were formed. We are made unique for a reason, and that is to fit the one-of-a-kind purpose, also uniquely designed for us. The truth is we are all beautiful. Human life is beautiful and the form of a human being is the most significant and wonderful thing.

When we embrace and love who we are, value the way we are made and care for ourselves, it shows our significance. We know we count for much. We know we are beautiful just the way we are, just the way we are meant to be; perfect for such a time as this.

Also, each of us has a one-of-a-kind personality. The way we love is one-of-a-kind. Our personal style and creativity is one-of-a-kind. How we communicate is different. How we write or give expression to something is unique. If a group of people were to write about the same topic, not one paper would be written the same. That is because our personal expression of life is unique and one-of-a-kind.

You matter! What you have to say matters. You are worth being cared about, listened to and validated. You are recognised. You are important.

laying the foundation.

ILLUSTRATION: MONA LISA

Use a paper copy of the Mona Lisa as an example of how much more the original is worth than a copy. The Mona Lisa is valuable because it is an original. Its value is reflected by the way it is treated. Any copy from the original is not worth the same as what the original is worth.

You are an original. Your worth comes from you being a one-off. You cannot be compared, cloned or replaced.

GROUP DISCUSSION: ONE-OF-A-KIND IS BEAUTIFUL!

Comparison is a real issue that many, if not all, women struggle with at one time or another.
EMBRACE – accept and love who you are.
CELEBRATE – enjoy the differences people have to offer.

We begin to compare ourselves to others when we feel inadequate or insecure about who we truly are. Our individuality carries great worth, and because of this we don't need to compare, change or modify who we are to fit the mould of someone else.

As a group, discuss the following questions:
1. What things do we compare ourselves to? What is unhealthy comparison?
2. What is the difference between comparison and being inspired by someone?
3. Who is someone you look up to? Are inspired by? Why?

Write the participants' responses on the board. The facilitator can share their personal examples if it will help with the group discussion.

presentation – 'value yourself because you are one-of-a-kind.'

ACTIVITY: STAYING FRESH AND HIGHLIGHTING YOUR SHINE

Discuss what 'staying fresh' means and how good it feels when skin and hair is clean. You may also want to talk about:
- Washing your hands before handling food items
- How to manage menstrual cycles
- Coaching on skin care (cleansing, moisturising, sunscreen, as well as skin types and how to handle acne), hygiene (deodorant, oral care) and hair care (shampoo, conditioning, styling)
- How marketing and magazines may form thoughts about beauty that lead to wearing make-up because you may not feel good about yourself
- Being breast-aware.[1]

Emphasise to the women that all these activities are simply basic health and beauty tips that can either be learnt from friends and magazines or in a classroom environment.

At the beginning of this activity, emphasise the uniqueness of each individual and the fact that we are all one-of-a-kind and that is what gives us worth. Then, divide the class into groups of four and distribute the resources. This can be done around one big cluster of tables.

For the face, this is a great opportunity to invite a skin care specialist to demonstrate the techniques on a willing student volunteer. Emphasise that the skin is the largest organ in the body and worth caring for.

Topics to cover include:
- A simple outline on what 'skin' is
- Different skin types and how to care for them
- The importance of water for healthy skin
- The importance of good nutrition for healthy skin
- A daily process of cleansing, moisturising and sunscreen
- Face masks – organic (homemade) or commercial
- Skin protection from sun damage
- The normality of skin changes and how to handle acne.

---

1 For more information, please view http://www.mcgrathfoundation.com.au/images/files/BreastAwareBrochureA4.pdf

ACTIVITY: GIVE EXPRESSION TO OUR ONE-OF-A-KIND FEATURES.

Handout photocopies of black and white faces (2 faces per woman). Encourage the women to colour in the faces with eye shadow and blush or coloured pens. For one face, ask the women to be as creative as they want. For the other face, ask the women to make a face with a more "natural" look. Once everyone has completed their pieces of art, encourage the women to look at each other's masterpieces. Discuss the fact that make-up is only used to enhance their beauty, as they are already beautiful from within. Make-up should not be used to cover up or change who we are or to be worn as a mask. Make-up as a function is to simply bring out and express our uniqueness. However, make-up can also create problems with image, if used to cover yourself up or if it gets to the point where you can't seem to live without it at all.

For hair care, this is a great opportunity to invite a hairdresser to demonstrate on a willing volunteer. However, cutting is not permitted. The topics to cover include:
- A great cut and style
- Shampooing and conditioning
- Perms and colour
- Helpful hints including the causes of stress on hair.

See Appendix C for a hair care handout.

discussion and wrap-up.

Q. What is a one-of-a-kind feature that you like about yourself?
Q. Why do you think living a one-of-a-kind life is important?

Women can often find it hard talking about what they like about themselves. Encourage them to push through. If someone is struggling to answer the question, ask the group if anyone wants to suggest a feature they admire about the person.

ASSESS OUTCOMES
Reinforce the WORTH concept. Affirm the group as a whole or to each individual by name – 'I am one-of-a-kind'.

shine factor.
IDEAS: Small hygiene packs

note to facilitator.
We would like to focus on homemade natural products as much as possible to make it fun, interesting and low cost. Avoid talking about 'good' and 'bad' skin. It really is all about feeling comfortable with the skin that belongs uniquely to each of us, i.e. colour, type, beauty spots, freckles, texture and complexion.'

'BODY AND SOUL, I AM WONDERFULLY MADE'

worth.

SESSION THREE | AM WONDERFULLY MADE

MATERIAL REQUIRED: Name badges, Shine factor, whiteboard markers, whiteboard
HEALTH MATERIALS: Examples of healthy food, recipes **ENERGY ITEMS:** Water bottle, sports trainers, t-shirts, sports hats, sports equipment, cardboard, pens.

Please see recommended layout below.

ACTIVITY	DETAILS	NOTES/MATERIALS
Icebreaker (10 mins)	Activity: WORTH acronym	RESORUCES: whiteboard, markers.
Power Focus (10 mins)	'I AM WONDERFULLY MADE' Illustration: A Teacup Story Illustration: Your value is priceless	RESORUCES: a teacup story handout (see Appendix J)
Laying The Foundation (20 mins)	Group Discussion: The body – wonderfully made! Describe all the different facets of the body, Discuss questions as a group.	
Presentation (40 mins)	ACTIVITY OPTIONS: Health Energy	Hand out any relevant information, Healthy foods on display, Equipment for activity.
Group Discussion and Wrap-up (10 mins)	Q. What have you learnt from today? Q. How would you describe worth in your own words? Reinforce Worth concept – 'I AM WONDERFULLY MADE'	
Shine Factor	As you give out the gifts, encourage each woman	Gifts

outcomes.
By the end of this session, each woman will be able to:

EXPLAIN HER UNDERSTANDING OF THE WORTH CONCEPT

IDENTIFY WAYS TO VALUE HERSELF

icebreaker.

ACTIVITY: WORTH ACRONYM

Have the participants pair up and come up with an acronym for WORTH.
Share their responses in the small group. For example:

W – Wonderful, Well-being
O – Original, One-of-a-kind
R – Real, Radiant
T – Treasured, Transforming
H – Healthy, Hope

power focus.
'I AM WONDERFULLY MADE'

There are many facets to who we are. Every part of us has a purpose and a function. Our mind, body, emotions, personality, character, passions and dreams are all intricate parts of us.

There are many characteristics that contribute to our individuality: our strengths, talents, laughter and smile have all been uniquely designed just for us. No one else is exactly the same. We have been designed just the way we are for a reason and a purpose. When we love something, we value it. Anything we love and adore, we treat with value. When we love ourselves, we are valuing ourselves.

The idea of living a life that shines is to see all we do, be about placing value on ourselves and others. We exercise to be strong in the core of our body so that we can be fit to carry on our amazing journey well. We require fuel for the body by eating the right food to keep healthy, as well as limiting chemicals where possible that are harmful for our inner and outer environment.

*Ask two to three girls
to volunteer to read a teacup story*
(See Appendix J)

A TEA CUP
story

A couple went into an antique shop one day and found a beautiful teacup sitting on a shelf. They took it off the shelf, so they could look at it more closely, and said, "We really want to buy this gorgeous cup."

All of the sudden, the teacup began to talk, saying, "I wasn't always like this. There was a time when I was just a cold, hard, colourless lump of clay. One day my master picked me up and said, 'I could do something with this.' Then he started to pat me, and roll me, and change my shape."

"I said, 'What are you doing? That hurts. I don't know if I want to look like this! Stop!' But he said, 'Not yet.'

"Then he put me on a wheel and began to spin me around and around and around, until I screamed, 'Let me off, I am getting dizzy!' 'Not yet,' he said.

"Then he shaped me into a cup and put me in a hot oven. I cried, 'Let me out! It's hot in here, I am suffocating.' But he just looked at me through that little glass window and smiled and said, 'Not yet.'

"When he took me out, I thought his work on me was over, but then he started to paint me. I couldn't believe what he did next. He put me back into the oven, and I said, 'You have to believe me, I can't stand this! Please let me out!' But he said, 'Not yet.'

"Finally, he took me out of the oven and set me up on a shelf where I thought he had forgotten me. Then one day he took me off the shelf and held me before a mirror. I couldn't believe my eyes, I had become a beautiful teacup that everyone wants to buy."

AUTHOR UNKNOWN

ILLUSTRATION: OUR VALUE IS PRICELESS

Human value is not determined by what people say about us. It's not determined by whether or not we have failed more times than we have succeeded. Our value is not determined by whether or not we have finished school, have a job, a car, a boyfriend or are well-liked. Circumstances like whether we are sick or healthy, rich or poor do not determine our value.

If our value is not determined by all these things, then what is it determined by? What price do we put on ourselves?

'We are all priceless.'

laying the foundation.

GROUP DISCUSSION: THE BODY – WONDERFULLY MADE!

Random facts about the body:
- The human heart creates enough pressure when it pumps blood out to the body, that it could squirt blood 30 feet!
- No two outer ears (pinnae) – even your own – are exactly alike. There are some key identification points on the outer ear that do not change throughout one's life. Earology is the study of the external ear which, like fingerprints, shows a unique design from person to person.
- Man's one kilogram brain is the most complex and orderly arrangement of matter known in the universe.
- The human eye can distinguish about 17,000 different colours.
- When you sneeze, all your bodily functions stop, even your heart. It is impossible to sneeze and keep your eyes open at the same time.

Ask the group to describe all the different facets of the body. Write up their answers up on the board.

- Mind: Mental capacity
- Organs: Heart, liver, lungs, stomach, intestines, kidneys, bladder
- Outer body: Skin, hair, nails
- Blood: Oxygen
- Physical mobility: Arms, legs, neck, back, feet, hands, muscles
- Emotions: Feelings
- Subconscious and conscious thoughts
- Knowledge: The brain stores up information throughout our lifetime
- Awareness of our surroundings (we need it to drive a car)
- Atmosphere: We hold the power to create the right atmosphere
- Personality: Character traits
- Attitude: Healthy or unhealthy attitudes towards self or others
- Expression: Sing, dance, body language, writing, talking, presentation.

Our body is the main vessel that allows us to function. When we are sick, it restricts our ability to do everyday things. We realise how much we need our body when we are limited in what we can do. When we are healthy, we feel like we can do anything. Our body enables us to do the things we love doing; having fun, enjoying the company of others, studying, travelling, exercising etc. Our body helps us to outwork our dreams and desires.

Q. Do we truly value and appreciate our bodies?
Q. If our bodies are valuable to us, how should we look after them?

EYES	No one has been born with the same kind of eye. In the movies, we see the use of a person's iris to help identify each individual. No one sees life the way we do. We hold a unique perspective, a unique vision.
FEET	No one lives the same story. No one has walked the journey that we have. There is value to our story. Our journey can bring hope to others.
HANDS	Think about what we use our hands for. There are so many different purposes. Our hands have touched the lives of others. How we display our care for others is unique from anyone else. Our hands and the story they bring have value.
HEART	The heart is tender, fragile and precious. The words we speak come from our heart. How we love others and how we treat others will impact their lives in a powerful way.
HEAD	Inside our head is a brain that contains intelligence, creativity, insight and our thoughts. The way we think and see life is different from anyone else. We carry unique perspectives and creative thoughts.
SOUL	Our soul is the very core of our being. It is our emotions and our thoughts. Our personality and each characteristic create our unique core. Our soul is custom made for our body.
MOUTH	The way we communicate with others is unique. We all have a unique way of talking and communicating that reflects our character and personality.

Each of us are masterpieces, one-of-a-kind, custom-built for a wonderful purpose. Every detail of who we are was carefully thought and designed uniquely. None of us are a mistake; we all have a purpose, a destination that only we can fulfil.

presentation.

OPTIONS: There are 2 options for this session, Health or Energy. Choose the activity that best suits your target audience and make it come alive by ensuring the presentation is relevant to your group.

ACTIVITY: HEALTH

You are about to embark on an adventure that will lead you to greater personal understanding, more energy and a greater zest for life.

1. Go through nutritional information with the women. Discuss:
    - Benefits of eating a balanced meal with lots of fruit and fibre and less processed foods
    - Vitamins we get from certain foods
    - Effects of unhealthy eating.

Ask the women to write down what they would eat on a weekly basis and discuss whether there are alternatives to unhealthy food.

2. For the health session, set the room up with colourful fruit platters for everyone, bottles of water and so forth. It is preferable to have a professional as your guest presenter for this activity, such as a nutritionist, doctor, nurse or health professional skilled in this area. We should not instruct on what we have no qualification for. You could also bring in a range of other different healthy foods for the women to try (such as dried fruit and nuts, cereal, vegetables and so forth) or make a smoothie or fresh juice with the women.
    * Check for allergies.

Always focus on health not image. We feel good when we are healthy. By eating healthy, we value our body.

ACTIVITY: ENERGY

1. Ask the women about what form of exercise they do. It's best to exercise daily, whether it's walking the dog for 30 minutes or playing a team sport. Our muscles need to be exercised to keep definition and remain strong. When we exercise we activate our happy endorphins, which help keep our emotions in balance.

2. Encourage the women to get involved in exercise activities such as Pilates, sit-ups, push-ups, stretches, lunges or exercises they can do with a partner.

These exercises need to be fun so that every woman wants to participate. Give women advance notice to bring in shorts and shoes for this activity. Note: Make sure that your participants are physically able to do these activities. Participants are welcome to not get involved in this activity if they are not comfortable. For the Energy session, set the room up with a fitness theme or like a gym class with yoga mats. Display fitness items such as water bottles, sports trainers, t-shirts, sports hats, and sports equipment (tennis racquets, tennis ball, basketball and so forth).

Invite a qualified fitness instructor to attend. Plan the session with them beforehand. Ensure that the focus is on *'looking after ourselves because we are valuable'*. Practise some exercises and draw up individual fitness plans for the women.

Overexercising is as harmful to our bodies as no exercise. Balance is the key. It is essential for our bodies to have regular rest days to revitalise and restore the muscles we use. It is also important to emphasise that health is the most important focus here. The benefits of healthy eating and exercise come when it is a regular part of our lifestyle.

Basic principles of health at every size are:
- Accept and respect diversity of body shapes and sizes
- Recognise health and well-being as multi-dimensional, including physical, social, spiritual, occupational, emotional and intellectual aspects
- Promote all aspects of health and well-being for all sizes
- Promote eating in a manner which balances individual nutritional needs, hunger and so forth
- Promote life-enhancing physical activity in tune with your body type [2]

shine factor.
IDEAS: Healthy food, bottled water, 'I AM WONDERFULLY MADE' quote, and a nutrition fact sheet scrolled up with a ribbon.

note to facilitator.
If you or any of the group members have any particular personal or health concerns (physical or emotional health) about a participant, we recommend you speak to a teacher or counsellor. If you are bringing in presenters, plan the activity with them beforehand. Provide any resources they might require: butcher's paper, pens, handouts, and photocopies. Pay close attention to any woman who requires some extra care and encouragement.

[2] Source: BodyMatters Australasia, www.bodymatters.com.au

'CHOOSE LIFE'

strength.

SESSION FOUR I HAVE THE POWER OF CHOICE
SESSION FIVE MY DECISIONS DETERMINE MY DESTINATION
SESSION SIX I HAVE RESILIENCE

BASIS. 'CHOOSE LIFE'
introduction.

Strength is the power within us that helps us rise above circumstances and adversity. Strength enables us to overcome our challenges. Life is not always smooth sailing. There will be some storms and high waves, as well as calm waters. How we face the storms of life will determine the effect that they have on us.

Being able to overcome adversity and challenges is not just for us but for everyone. Our story of challenge and triumph can give hope and strength to others in situations similar to ours. Strength is for service.

Strength is like a muscle. If we don't use it, it will remain dormant, idle, unused.
By using the strength within us, we are building and growing it, as well as our character and personhood.

Many of us carry around 'emotional' things that can weigh us down like heavy coats and bags. These weights are the baggage from our lives; the hurt, the pain, and the regrets. We have the choice to receive healing from our issues and to let go of our baggage.

Strength is exercising our power to choose. By exercising choices that help us live 'balanced', we build and develop our inner strength.

The Strength concept explores:

thoughts. feelings. choices.

i have the power of CHOICE.

We have a free will – the power to make choices in our lives. Our strength grows when we exercise our will for good, for ourselves and for others.

Choices affect our lives and the lives of people around us. No matter how we feel, we have the power to choose our direction in life. This does not mean choices will always be easy. Some of our choices will challenge the very core of who we believe we are. Making right choices in life, especially in difficult situations, builds our strength and our maturity as women. Our decisions can be influenced by others, especially those we love. We can choose to hand our 'power of choice' over to them or we can hold onto it.

We can choose to make each of our experiences in life count. We can't always change our circumstances, but we can take control over what we do about them.

We have the CHOICE to: RESPOND to a situation or REACT to it.

Above everything, we hold the power to choose.

my decisions determine my
DESTINATION.

In every situation, in every day, we make choices. In those choices there are consequences that add to our life, moving us forward and there are consequences that stop us moving at all or cause us to move backwards. There are decisions that can fast track us on our journey and others that can keep us from our desired destination. Decisions we make give us control over our life, but they don't just affect our life, they also impact the people around us. There are choices that are selfish and those that are selfless.

All the decisions we make – from getting out of bed each morning to who we marry – have consequences. Our choices determine what our tomorrow will look like. Things we decide to overcome and things we decide to accept all have a direct effect on our life. Often we don't realise that it's the small, everyday decisions that get us to our desired destination.

i have RESILIENCE.

A strong person is able to stand firm whilst facing significant difficulties, as they have a strong sense of self-belief and faith to keep calm and carry on.

KEY MESSAGE TO REINFORCE THROUGH STRENGTH SESSIONS:

*i have strength! i have the power of choice!
my decisions determine my destination! i have resilience!*

'CHOOSE LIFE'

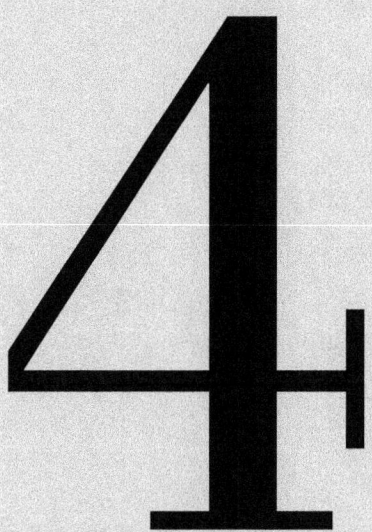

strength.

SESSION FOUR | HAVE THE POWER OF CHOICE

MATERIAL REQUIRED: Feelings cards (See Appendix D), fizzy drink bottle, heart shaped paper, whiteboard and markers, mirror, 'Stop, Think, Choose' cards (See Appendix D), pens and permanent markers, name badges, 'I have the power of choice' handout (See Appendix D).

Please see recommended layout below.

ACTIVITY	DETAILS	NOTES/MATERIALS
Icebreaker (10 mins)	Activity: Understanding love languages	RESOURCES: Love heart shaped paper.
Power Focus (5 mins)	Group Discussion: What is strength? 'I HAVE THE POWER OF CHOICE.'	
Laying The Foundation (10 mins)	Emotions defined and explained	RESOURCES: Mirror
Presentation (60 mins)	Group activity: Identifying feelings Discussion: Managing our emotions Demonstration: Fizzy drink bottle Group activity: 'Stop, Think, Choose' Problem-solving	RESOURCES: Feelings cards, Fizzy drink bottle, 'Stop, Think, Choose' cards, blank paper & pens.
Group Discussion and Wrap-up (5 mins)	Discuss how we can strengthen the balance of our emotions so we can live a healthy lifestyle. Reinforce Strength concept – 'I HAVE THE POWER OF CHOICE'	
Shine Factor	As you give out the gifts, encourage each woman	Gifts

outcomes.
By the end of this session, each woman will be able to:

EXPLORE AND UNDERSTAND THAT EVERY WOMAN IS BORN WITH FEELINGS

DEMONSTRATE SKILLS REQUIRED TO ENHANCE THE POWER OF CHOICE

icebreaker.
ACTIVITY: UNDERSTANDING LOVE LANGUAGES

Hand out one heart card (simply cut out some paper heart cards) to every participant. Then ask the participants to choose which of the primary love languages best fits them. This is a helpful message, as it is important that the participants know that people have a different way of expressing and receiving love.

Ask everyone to write one thing that makes them feel happy or feel loved without showing the next person. Then on the other side of the heart, have the participant write their name and hand it over to you.

This is a test of how well we all know each other. Once the answer has been mentioned, the participants have to try and guess who it is - it could be anyone in the room. Understanding our love language and the love language of the people around us helps us to understand each other and show love to others in a way that enables them to see they are loved. Your love language will differ from the people in your life. Each of us speaks and understands one that makes it easy for us to feel loved. If you try to communicate using only your native language, it may be foreign to other people. To be understood, you need to know and speak your friend's love language.

power focus.

GROUP DISCUSSION: ASK THE WOMEN WHAT THEY THINK STRENGTH IS.

'I have the power of choice.'

We have free will – the power to make choices in our lives. Our strength grows when we exercise our will for good, for ourselves and for others.

Choices affect our lives and the lives of people around us. No matter how we feel, we have the power to choose our direction in life. This does not mean choices will always be easy. Some of our choices will challenge the very core of who we believe we are. Yet others will be easy. Making right choices in life, especially in difficult situations, builds our strength and our maturity as women. Our decisions can be influenced by others, especially those we love. We can choose to hand our 'power of choice' over to them or we can hold onto it.

We can choose to make each of our experiences in life count. We can't always change our circumstances, but we can take control over what we do about them.

We have the CHOICE to: RESPOND to a situation or REACT to it.
Above everything, we hold the power to choose.

laying the foundation.

EMOTION | ih-moh-sh*uh* n |
Any strong feeling, such as joy or fear, the part of a person's character based on feelings rather than thought.
It's important to recognise how we are feeling.

1. DEFINE WHAT EMOTIONS ARE : Ask the women to close their eyes and picture going on a journey toward your desired destination. There are mountains and hills rising up challenging the path they have chosen. Ask the women to open their eyes and open discussion explaining that, often these mountains or hills can be our feelings and we can be unsure of how to navigate our way through them.

2. EXPLAIN THAT EMOTIONS ARE HEALTHY: Imagine going through life without feeling anything. Discuss what that would look like for each woman. Feelings give life richness and depth. All our emotions are a healthy indicator as to how we are feeling. We can feel different emotions each hour of the day! Each feeling we have tells us what is happening on the inside. We may feel angry, sad, joyful, hopeful or peaceful. They all play a role in the makeup of who we are. It's important to recognise how we are feeling. They are keys to revealing what we think about things - our mindsets and our belief systems. What we think and subsequently feel influences the decisions we make and how we live out our life.

THOUGHTS & BELIEFS • FEELINGS • DECISIONS • RESPONSE

All these things influence our behaviours and actions.

Our thoughts and beliefs influence our feelings, which influence our decision-making. These in turn influence our responses to situations. Feelings should not be ignored or buried. Instead, as we honestly accept our feelings we begin to mature as women. When we identify and acknowledge these feelings it starts the process of disempowering the desire to react so that we can respond to what is happening around us.

3. MIRROR EXPLANATION: Our emotions are not wrong; they are an integral part of who we are. Our emotions are a mirror to ourselves and what's going on inside. Encourage the women to take some time to look, but be aware that it goes against some cultural traditions to stare into the mirror.

Q. If the women were to look in the mirror, what would they see?

How we feel does not shape who we are – for example, 'I feel useless, therefore I am useless'. How we are feeling is not joined to our value of self. Understanding what our feelings are telling us helps us to create a balanced and healthy lifestyle. Spend a few minutes reaffirming the value of feelings, acknowledging the important role they play in our life.

presentation.
GROUP ACTIVITY: IDENTIFYING FEELINGS

Who has ever been asked 'How are you?' and your reply was 'I don't know'? Who has ever found themselves crying for no reason? It's important to understand how and why we are feeling this way. There are four basic feelings each of us has:

FEAR: Fear is a normal emotion. It tells us there may be danger close by. There are times where fear protects us, but there are also times when fear can keep us from moving forward.

HAPPINESS: We enjoy who we are and where we are at when we are happy with life. It's good to sometimes stop and say out loud 'I am happy today!'

ANGER: Our anger is normal and a healthy emotion. It becomes unhealthy when it is used to hurt others (verbally, emotionally and physically). There is a big difference between anger and abuse. Anger tells us that there is an issue or a hurt that needs to be resolved.

If we hurt others or others hurt us through anger, seek out professionals or a trusted adult who can help – such as a local GP, counsellor or psychologist.

SADNESS: It's okay to cry. It's natural. It is not a sign of weakness – in fact, it can express how we are feeling when words cannot. It can also release some pressure or stress that we may be feeling. When we find it hard to stop being sad or when we stop doing things we love, then it is important to seek out professional help to assist us to understand why we are feeling sad all the time.

a) Which of the four primary feelings make up the following feelings? Give out cards with different emotions on them. The women then need to categorise the emotions under the headings: ANGRY, HAPPY, SAD, FEARFUL, COMBINATION. (See Appendix D for feelings cards).

PRIMARY FEELING	ANGRY	HAPPY	SAD	FEARFUL	COMBINATION
FEELINGS	*Furious*	*Excited*	*Aggrieved*	*Nervous*	*Guilty*
	Irritated	*Satisfied*	*Miserable*	*Terrified*	*Jealous*
	Annoyed	*Pleased*	*Down*	*Anxious*	*Ashamed*
	Ticked off	*Joyful*	*Disappointed*	*Worried*	*Embarrassed*
	Humiliated	*Delighted*	*Hurt*	*Concerned*	*Uncomfortable*
	Frustrated	*Comfortable*	*Lonely*	*Afraid*	*Confused*
	Hurt	*Hopeful*	*Forgotten*	*Uncertain*	*Torn*
	Sarcastic	*Surprised*	*Remorseful*	*Out of control*	*Envious*
	Disgusted	*Positive*	*Rejected*	*Uneasy*	*Compassionate*

b) Feelings Statements

EG 1: **STATEMENT: I FEEL EMBARRASSED.**
Q. When you feel embarrassed, are you feeling more sad, fearful or angry?
A. Probably angry about the position I am in right now and scared that I might make a mistake.

EG 2: **STATEMENT: I FEEL JEALOUS.**
Q. When you feel jealous, are you feeling more sad, fearful or angry?
A. More scared that I'll lose someone I care about and fearful that my partner may not be telling me the truth.

EG 3: **STATEMENT: I FEEL DOWN.**
Q. When you feel down, are you feeling more sad, fearful or angry?
A. I'm feeling sad and confused about why I am sad

Read out feeling statements one at a time then ask the 'question', encouraging the group to discuss what they feel when hearing the statements. They may feel different emotions to the ones in the 'answer' and that's OK. There are no wrong answers. We are all unique women with unique experiences which make up the reasons why we feel certain emotions stronger than others.

DISCUSSION: MANAGING OUR EMOTIONS

It's important to maintain a balance when it comes to our emotions and not live a life controlled by them. Our emotions can become like a rollercoaster. If we allow our feelings to get out of balance they can begin to run our lives. In order to keep ourselves balanced we use our emotions to tell us how we are feeling, instead of allowing them to influence our choices in life.

Once we identify our feelings, it may be helpful to explore them further:
- Why am I feeling like this?
- How can I resolve this?
- What has caused these feelings?
- How long have I felt this way?
- What choices do I have?
- Can I change how I am feeling?
- Do I need to forgive someone?

For example: If you're feeling angry, ask yourself:
- 'Why am I angry?'
- 'What has caused this anger?'
- 'Where is this coming from?'
- 'How long has this made me angry?'

When we begin to explore our feelings and the reasons behind them, we start to understand our past and our present and look forward to a different future.

DEMONSTRATION: FIZZY DRINK BOTTLE

When a fizzy drink bottle is shaken and the lid is taken off, the fizzy drink bottle explodes out of the bottle. Our emotions can do the same thing. They can explode over something that we would normally not get upset over. Our emotions have the potential to dramatically influence all aspects of our life, the choices we make and the kinds of relationships we form.

Instead of taking the lid off as soon as you have shaken the fizzy drink bottle, let the bubbles go down for a while and then remove the lid. The same goes for our emotions. If possible, leave the room until the emotions calm down and then come back to find a resolution.

Encourage the group to discuss how they keep their emotions balanced in life.

GROUP ACTIVITY: STOP, THINK, CHOOSE

Q. How do I feel today?... In the middle of the circle on the floor, put out different emotion cards. When the women are seated, have them pick up the words that reflect their feelings 'today'. Discuss why they chose these feelings.

PURPOSE: For women to begin the process of identifying and acknowledging what she is feeling.

WE CAN RESPOND, RATHER THAN REACT.

When we identify our feelings it allows us to take a step back from reacting and gives us time to respond in a healthy way to the situation.

We have two ways to deal with any situation:

RESPOND Take the time to digest what is happening and discover a solution that is best for everyone.

REACT Our emotions are given power to react in the situation before we have the time to think. This sometimes leads to regret or feelings of guilt after the event.

We can't always change the circumstances, but we can take control over what we do in the circumstances. We can choose how we want to behave.

Set the room up with 3 stations. Label each station 'STOP', 'THINK' and 'CHOOSE'.
Hand out 3 cards to each woman: 1) STOP 2) THINK 3) CHOOSE

'STOP' STATION
Give women some paper and a pen to write down an issue, situation or decision they want to make. At this station show the women some breathing exercises. Emphasise that before we react to our circumstances, we can stop. The breathing exercise is a practical skill that can remind them to 'stop'.

'THINK' STATION
Ask women to write down their choices to the issue, situation or decision they have chosen to explore. This station demonstrates the process before acting on a decision.

At this station, we begin to think through our choices and the consequences of each choice, and then decide on the best option. This process actually makes the decision at the 'Choose' station much easier, because we have decided in advance what we can do.

'CHOOSE' STATION
Ask the women to circle the option that best suits the outcome they want.
At this station women get to enjoy the 'fruit' (impact or consequence) of their decision.

Ask the group to sit down and discuss the process of making healthy choices. Give some real life examples.
- What are some healthy choices we can make?
- We choose our behaviour, others don't control how we respond or react.

PURPOSE: To slow down the reaction time and strengthen the response time.

When we respond to our situations we are respecting ourselves and others.
Respect gives value to ourselves. When we make healthy choices, we place value on ourselves and others.

'You can FEEL and then REACT... OR...
You can FEEL, STOP, THINK and CHOOSE.'

PROBLEM-SOLVING EXERCISES

These topics can be discussed as a large group or in small groups. A scribe can be appointed to record ideas from the discussion, which can then be shared with the whole group. Butcher's paper is useful for this.

PROBLEM | prob-*luh* m |
A recurring feeling of discomfort; any question or matter involving doubt, uncertainty, or difficulty; a state of difficulty that needs to be resolved.

FOR PROBLEMS YOU CAN CHANGE
PROBLEM-FOCUSED COPING
- Define the problem
- List all possible solutions
- Assess each possible solution to the problem
- Plan how to implement the solution
- Implement plan and review progress
- Journaling

FOR PROBLEMS YOU CAN'T CHANGE
EMOTION-FOCUSED COPING
- Positive reappraisal – e.g. 'Well, at least I learnt something'
- Distraction
- Planning pleasant activities
- Social support
- Relaxation
- Positive self-statements and affirmations, such as 'I can get through this'[3]

---

3   Source: Body Matters Australasia, www.bodymatters.com.au

discussion and wrap-up.
Discuss how we can strengthen the balance of our emotions so that we can live a healthy lifestyle. For example:

- Listen to upbeat music or classical, soothing instrumentals.
- Make a choice every day to respond rather than react.
- Take time each day to do something just for ourselves.
- Begin the day speaking something positive about ourselves.

ASSESS OUTCOMES
Reinforce the Strength concept. Affirm the group as a whole or to each individual by name, 'I have the power of choice.' This exercise is a powerful way to end a session.

shine factor.
IDEAS: Affirmation card – write something encouraging for each woman that you have observed.

note to facilitator.
See Appendix D for handouts.
Look out for women who may need extra care and encouragement.
Set the room up differently today. Create a new mood. Develop a sense of intimacy, connectedness and creative space. One thing you could do is remove the middle table and have the chairs in a circle to create a more intimate atmosphere. Use these Strength sessions to stimulate discussion amongst your group.

'CHOOSE LIFE'

5
strength.

SESSION FIVE MY DECISIONS DETERMINE MY DESTINATION

MATERIAL REQUIRED: 'Qualities' flash cards, whiteboard markers, whiteboard, pens and permanent markers, name badges, Diamond and Journey of a Diamond handout (see Appendix E), blank paper.

Please see recommended layout below.

ACTIVITY	DETAILS	NOTES/MATERIALS
Icebreaker (10 mins)	Activity: Put-ups	
Power Focus (5 mins)	'MY DECISIONS DETERMINE MY DESTINATION.'	
Laying The Foundation (10 mins)	Illustration: Diamonds	RESOURCES: Diamond, Journey of a Diamond handout.
Presentation (60 mins)	OPTIONS: Activity: Convictions Group discussion: Boundaries Activity: Respect	RESOURCES: Paper, pens, permanent markers.
Group Discussion and Wrap-up (5 mins)	Q. What qualities are important to you? Q. What have you discovered about yourself today? Reinforce Strength concept – 'MY DECISIONS DETERMINE MY DESTINATION'	
Shine Factor	As you give out the gifts, encourage each woman	Gifts

outcomes.

By the end of this session, each woman will be able to:

APPLY AND PRACTISE DECISION-MAKING SKILLS

RECOGNISE THE VALUE OF RESPECT AND BOUNDARIES

icebreaker.
ACTIVITY: PUT-UPS

'Put ups' are the opposite of 'put-downs'.
We purposefully choose to speak 'courage' to each other face-to-face.

STAGE 1: Speaker has eye contact with the person they are about to 'put-up'.
STAGE 2: The person receiving the 'put-up' can only say 'thank you'.

This activity is designed to give and receive encouragement. It can be very foreign and awkward for women to affirm each other face-to-face. Be prepared to lead the way, be genuine and gentle. Ensure everyone has a turn. For alternative icebreakers see Appendix A.

power focus.
STRENGTH COMES IN TWO STAGES:

1. Choice – We hold the power to choose
2. Consequences to our decisions – Decisions determine our destination.

'My decisions determine my destination.'

In every situation, in every day, we make choices. In those choices there are consequences that add to our life moving us forward, and there are consequences that stop us moving at all or cause us to move backwards.

There are decisions that can fast track us on our journey and others that can keep us from it.

Decisions we make give us control over our life; but they don't just affect our life, they also impact the people around us. There are choices that are selfish and those that are selfless.

All the decisions we make – from getting out of bed each morning to who we marry –have consequences. Our choices determine what our tomorrow will look like. Things we decide to overcome and things we decide to accept all have a direct effect on our life. Often we don't realise that it's the small, everyday decisions that get us to our desired destination.

laying the foundation.
ILLUSTRATION: DIAMONDS

Diamonds are the strongest substance on earth. Extreme levels of heat and pressure produce a diamond. The more intense the pressure, the larger the diamond becomes. Diamonds have great value and strength. The only thing that can cut a diamond is another diamond. Once the uncut diamond is formed, it begins the journey towards the earth's surface.

In its raw state, a diamond's potential is limitless. No matter what state you believe you are in, you are valuable like an uncut diamond. Think about the concept of a diamond polishing another diamond. When we position ourselves around other 'diamonds', they bring out the good in us. Diamonds can be positive mentors or people living with healthy boundaries.

Q. Can the journey of a diamond relate to the journey we have in our own lives?
Q. If you were handed a rock, would you think that it could be a diamond?

We can become diamonds through our choices. The rock was originally designed to be a diamond. The potential of the rock is realised through the diamond journey.

Let us not overlook the potential inside each one of us. Although believing in our own potential may be scary sometimes, it is when we make those decisions to release our potential that we grow stronger each day.

presentation. *Choose the activity that you think is most appropriate to your group.

CONVICTION | kuh n-vik-shuh n |
A fixed or firm, strong belief.

ACTIVITY: CONVICTIONS

Convictions are what we believe to be important to us.

Convictions help us with our decision making. Before we make a decision, we can think about whether it is in line with our convictions. There is a reason why we live with convictions. For example, I have a conviction about completing school because I want to have a good education and set myself up for the future.

Q. What are your convictions? Brainstorm the different convictions you have about:

- Relationships
- Respect
- Reputation
- Health
- Personal characteristics – integrity, honesty, faithfulness
- Achieving dreams.

Convictions are formed from our beliefs and value system. When we make decisions based on our convictions, we are showing others what we believe and value in life. This brings us to discuss the importance of having boundaries in place to allow our convictions to help us in deciding our destination.

GROUP DISCUSSION: BOUNDARIES

We may hear certain people talk about 'personal boundaries' from time to time. Indeed, boundaries are essential to cultivating a healthy sense of personal worth.

Q. How do we set up healthy boundaries?

Boundaries are like maps that show us where we start and finish. Some examples of boundaries in the world include property lines and state borders. Personal boundaries are similar to this. As unique individuals, we each need boundaries for our body, soul and heart to stay healthy.

Boundaries help us take care of our property – we hold onto the things that help us inside our fences and keep things that will hurt us outside. In short, boundaries help us keep the good in and the bad out. Boundaries also help us build a community, and within that community, everyone has their own space and property. The important idea to remember is that our gates must be flexible enough to allow or prevent entry of influences as we determine.

Some of us have lived a life where we have followed the demands or opinions of others in order to be 'nice people'. As a result, we may have lost ourselves in our efforts to please others and win their approval. Living this way allows frustration, abuse, depression or resentment to take root in our thoughts and emotions.

'Do you believe you have something valuable to offer the world?'

LET'S BEGIN

Building a life that contains healthy boundaries takes time and will always be a work in progress. It can seem to be a very long journey, but keep in mind that the journey moves forward when we take one step at a time. Take some time to reflect on where important boundaries need to be established and think about how to put them into practice. Form some discussion on the fact that boundaries are not an attempt to control another human being – although some of the people who you set boundaries with will certainly accuse you of that – it is a part of the process of defining ourselves and what is acceptable to us. Learning to set boundaries is vital to learning to love ourselves, and to communicating to others that we have worth.

POWER OF CHOICE
Even with life events that occur in a way that we seemingly don't have a choice over (being laid off work, the car breaking down, a flood, etc.) we still have a choice over how we respond to those events because we know what our boundaries are. We can choose to see things that feel like, and seem to be, tragic as opportunities for growth. Learning to set boundaries is a vital part of learning to communicate in a direct and honest manner. If you have a boundary that involves another person, you need to both agree on this boundary, value it and be accountable.

ACTIVITY: RESPECT

RESPECT | ri-spekt |
Esteem for or a sense of the worth or excellence of a person, the condition of being esteemed or honoured, to show regard or consideration for.

HONOUR | on-er |
The state of being honoured; the quality of being honourable and having a good name.
Giving worth and weight to what is truly valuable.

WHAT RESPECT IS

On a practical level, respect includes taking someone's feelings, needs, thoughts, ideas, wishes and preferences into consideration. It means taking all of these seriously and giving them worth and value. In fact, giving someone respect seems similar to valuing them and their thoughts, feelings and so forth. It also includes acknowledging them, listening to them, being truthful with them, and accepting their individuality.

Respect can be shown through behaviour and it can also be felt. We can act in ways which are considered respectful, yet we can also feel respect for someone and feel respected by someone. Because it is possible to act in ways that do not reflect how we really feel, the feeling of respect is more important than the behaviour without the feeling. When the feeling is there, the behaviour will naturally follow.

Respecting someone means also respecting their feelings. Here are ways to show respect:
- Asking them how they feel
- Validating their feelings
- Empathising with them
- Seeking understanding of their feelings
- Taking their feelings into consideration.

INDIVIDUALS OR IN PAIRS – Mind map ways to respect and honour yourself and others. For example, how do you honour the gift of your hands and how do you treat your body with honour? Or how do you honour your parents by valuing the fact that they brought you into the world and so forth? See 'How to Mind Map' by Tony Buzan for examples of mind maps.

*Make this session creative using coloured pens, cardboard and so forth.

discussion and wrap-up.

Q. What personal qualities are important to you?
Display all the cards out for the women to see. Encourage them to choose which cards are relevant to them.

Compassion	Integrity	Courage	Hospitality
Confidence	Joy	Forgiveness	Listening Skills
Creativity	Kindness	Teachability	Dreamer/Visionary
Encouragement	Trustworthiness	Patience	Peace
Enthusiasm	Determination	Motivation	
Excellence	Self-control	Wisdom	
Honesty	Passion	Generosity	

Add your own…
Alternative discussion questions: Q. What qualities come naturally to you?   Q. What kind of qualities would you like to develop? Q. What have you discovered about yourself today?

ASSESS OUTCOMES
Reinforce Strength concept. Affirm the group as a whole or to each individual by name –'My decisions determine my destiny.' This exercise is a powerful way to end a session.

shine factor.
IDEAS: Pearl bracelets or a handmade bracelet with beads. If you can find alphabet beads, have the word "shine" as part of the bracelet.

note to facilitator.
Look out for women who may need extra care and encouragement.

'CHOOSE LIFE'

6
strength.

SESSION SIX | HAVE RESILIENCE

MATERIAL REQUIRED: Paper, coloured pens/pencils, ball, DVD for movie scene, DVD player and TV, whiteboard markers, whiteboard.

Please see recommended layout below.

ACTIVITY	DETAILS	NOTES/MATERIALS
Icebreaker (10 mins)	Activity: Is pain good or bad?	RESOURCES: Whiteboard and whiteboard markers.
Power Focus (10 mins)	Group Discussion: What does resilience look like to you?	
Laying the Foundation (5 mins)	RESILIENCE	
Presentation (60 mins)	Demonstration: Movie Scene Group Discussion: Resilience Demonstration: Throw a ball Activity: Personal reflection	RESOURCES: DVD player and TV, DVD, ball, paper.
Group Discussion and Wrap-up (5 mins)	Q. What have you learnt today that you can practically apply to your life now?	
Shine Factor	As you give out the gifts, encourage each woman	Gifts

outcomes.
By the end of this session, each woman will be able to:
RECOGNISE THE VALUE OF DEVELOPING RESILIENCE

icebreaker.
ACTIVITY: IS PAIN GOOD OR BAD?
Split the group into two. One group will discuss how pain can be good and the other group will discuss how pain is bad. Then discuss as a whole the different answers the two groups discovered.

power focus.

Get into small groups and discuss what you believe resilience is and what it looks like to the women. Then bring the group back together and write the answers on the whiteboard, encouraging the women that there are no wrong answers as it could be individual to the person.

laying the foundation... Resilience

RESILIENCE | ri-zil-ee-*uh* ns |
The ability to recover readily from adversity.

Resilience is the strength to withstand adversity. It is the ability to handle difficult situations, people, environments and setbacks. Being able to bounce back and recover from adversity makes us stronger and contributes to our dreams becoming a reality. A resilient person is able to stand firm whilst facing significant difficulties and stress as they have a strong sense of self-belief and faith in their capabilities.

We need to understand that life will not always be smooth sailing. Life is not always great. Things happen that we would prefer didn't. But if life was always wonderful, would we appreciate all the great things or would we take them for granted? We can learn so much about ourselves when we go through challenges and problems. It is never comfortable when you're in the middle of adversity or challenge, but when you get through it, you can look back and see what you have learnt from the situation. Any mistakes we make are simply an opportunity to grow and learn.

presentation.
DEMONSTRATION: MOVIE SCENE
Choose a movie that displays a character that has overcome adversity and developed resilience. Show a few scenes that display their experience of adversity and resilience to explain this concept further. Suggested movies that relate to resilience are The Pursuit of Happyness, The Blind Side, and Not Without My Daughter.

GROUP DISCUSSION:

Q. What are some challenges you face each day?

- Peer pressure
- Losing a loved one/family breakdown
- Negative self-talk
- Rejection
- Addictions and substance use
- Loneliness

Q. How can you increase your resilience?

- Healthy relationships
- Participation
- Communication (someone to talk to)
- Overcoming problems, not giving up
- Standing up for what you believe
- Taking healthy risks
- Facing rejection or setbacks and trying again
- Not taking things personally
- Learning from your failures
- Getting information to understand what you're facing
- Adapting to new situations easily
- Being honest about your fears
- Figuring out who you are and what you want out of life, and not giving up on it
- Persevering no matter what
- Spending time with people who handle stress well.

'Start believing in what you can offer.'

DEMONSTRATION: THROW A BALL

Get two women to come out to the front. Have one woman throw the ball at the other woman (underarm throw). Her first reaction would be to catch the ball. Often our first instance is to accept the experiences that have happened to us and allow them to become part of our identity. We all have the choice to either ACCEPT or OVERCOME adversity, to act or react to our situations.

Now have the woman fold her arms and when the ball is thrown to her it should bounce off her. In this scenario she exercised the power of choice and allowed the ball to roll off her.

Reiterate the point from the first strength session that we can choose our responses to our situations.

ACTIVITY: PERSONAL REFLECTION

OPTION I: Distribute a piece of paper and pen to each woman. On one side of the paper write down 'Where I have persevered' and on the other side of the paper write down 'Where I have given up'. Encourage the group to spend some time writing down their personal answers.

OR

OPTION II: Write down a list of positive achievements you have accomplished and a list of difficult experiences you have overcome or survived.

After they have done this, bring the group back together and ask if anyone wants to share about what they have written. Explore what the woman have gained from persevering and if anything was gained from giving up. Use this to build and encourage the group to stay motivated when facing difficult situations. As the facilitator, be prepared to start the discussion off first. Encourage the group that if and when they face tough challenges in their life – it's important to talk about it with someone they trust. Planning and problem-solving challenges can help us overcome.

We can't do life alone. We need each other.

small group discussion.

Q. What have you learnt today that you can practically apply to your life now?

ASSESS OUTCOMES: Reinforce Strength concept. Affirm the group as a whole or to each individual by name –'I have resilience.' This exercise is a powerful way to end a session.

shine factor.

IDEAS: Have the words relating to Strength already written out on a smooth stone

note to the facilitator.

Remember, every participant's response is always valid; never publicly shame an answer and always look for the positive.

'I HAVE A HOPE AND A FUTURE'

P

purpose.

SESSION SEVEN MY POTENTIAL IS LIMITLESS
SESSION EIGHT MY LIFE HAS PURPOSE
SESSION NINE SHINE!

BASIS. 'I HAVE A HOPE AND A FUTURE.'

introduction.

The torment of purposelessness can tear a person apart. As Archbishop Desmond Tutu says, 'We humans can tolerate suffering but we cannot tolerate meaninglessness.' Everyone yearns to live a life that is significant. We often go through the motions of life getting caught up in the busyness, which can cause us to neglect our purpose; the 'something' we are passionate about that lies inside each and every one of us.

'Our passions are what make our heart sing.'

Our passions are linked to and help us identify and complete our purpose; what we were created for. As we begin to discover and live our life with purpose, we become less discouraged about where we are heading in life.

We were not created to live our lives alone. We need friends who help prepare us for the challenges ahead and who are committed to walk through them with us. Nothing can substitute friendships and interpersonal communication. Gathering together with like-minded people who spur us on and encourage us to not give up on our dreams helps us when we are feeling disheartened or discouraged. We can start discovering our purpose now.

'Don't despise the days of small beginnings!'

THE PURPOSE CONCEPT EXPLORES:

my potential is

LIMITLESS

Potential is what we are capable of becoming in every area of our life. This can include friends, family, career, health, finances, personal character and attitude. Our potential is limitless. Our potential is often in seed form. The seeds inside us are limitless. Each seed has the potential to grow and become everything it was designed to be. The only thing that can limit us from becoming all that we can be is <u>us</u>. Living in our potential requires believing in ourselves and being confident in who we are. Our potential will not grow or be realised unless we choose to put it into action.

What do you believe about yourself?

my life has PURPOSE.

We are unique; there is no one else like us. How we are designed, our passions, our talents, and our strengths are unique to each of us and have purpose. There is a blueprint inside all of us. We are purpose-built and exist for a reason. There is a purpose for our life.

Discovering our purpose is a key aspect to every person's journey. We get a taste of our purpose when we tap into the desires of our heart. What satisfies us and what makes us frustrated? We each have a specific wiring with a palette of gifts and strengths that are as unique to each individual as a thumbprint!

Developing our gifts and talents, identifying our dreams and desires and learning how to use them, all help us to live a life of purpose. Purpose enables us to make a difference in our world. Life does not have to be about just living for ourselves. Our life can be used to make a difference for others.

We can choose to live in a world that is about ourselves or we can choose to include others in our world where we can make a difference.

**KEY MESSAGE TO REINFORCE
THROUGH PURPOSE SESSIONS**

*my potential is limitless!
my life has purpose!*

'I HAVE A HOPE AND A FUTURE'

purpose.
SESSION SEVEN MY POTENTIAL IS LIMITLESS

MATERIAL REQUIRED: Potting and seed mix, polystyrene cups, water, walkway, music, apple seeds, name badges, whiteboard markers, whiteboard pens, coloured pencils, permanent markers, paper.

Please see recommended layout below.

ACTIVITY	DETAILS	NOTES/MATERIALS
Icebreaker (15 mins)	Activity: Walking tall	RESOURCES: a walkway, appropriate upbeat music
Power Focus (10 mins)	'MY POTENTIAL IS LIMITLESS'	RESOURCES: apple seed.
Laying The Foundation (10 mins)	Group Discussion: Seeds of greatness	RESOURCES: whiteboard, whiteboard marker.
Presentation (50 mins)	Activities: Planting a seed, Choosing confidence	RESOURCES: potting mix, seed, water, cup, walkway, music, paper.
Group Discussion and Wrap-up (5 mins)	Q. What can you do with these seeds starting today? Reinforce Purpose concept 'MY POTENTIAL IS LIMITLESS'	
Shine Factor	As you give out the gifts, encourage each woman	Gifts

outcomes.
By the end of this session, each woman will be able to:
RECOGNISE THE VALUE OF A POSITIVE ENVIRONMENT FOR HER POTENTIAL TO GROW
IDENTIFY WAYS TO BUILD HER CONFIDENCE

icebreaker.
ACTIVITY: WALKING TALL
Invite the group to stand and encourage each one to participate in the following exercise.
- Close your eyes and imagine that you are walking towards your dreams. By doing something different, we are learning more about us – our limits and our capabilities. We are expanding our capacity to meet challenges head on.
- Only have one woman at a time walking tall on the walkway. When the women get to the end of the walkway, encourage them to declare 'My potential is limitless'.
- The rest of the group is the encouraging cheer squad applauding each woman.

STEPS TO WALKING TALL
Step 1: Breathe in deeply through your nose until you feel your stomach and diaphragm swell. Now slowly contract your stomach from your pelvis to your rib cage and breathe slowly out through your mouth.

Step 2: Hold your shoulders back, tighten your bottom and straighten your back. Now look straight ahead at eye level so that your head is evenly poised above the spine and is at a right angle position to your neck.

power focus.
'MY POTENTIAL IS LIMITLESS'

What is potential?

POTENTIAL

| p*uh*-ten-sh*uh* l |
Possible, capable of being or becoming.

Potential is what we are capable of becoming in every area of our life. This can include friends, family, career, health, finances, personal character and attitude.
Our potential is limitless. Our potential is often in seed form. The seeds inside us are limitless.
Each seed has potential to grow and become everything it was designed to be.

The only thing that can limit us from becoming all that we can be is <u>ourselves.</u>

Living in our potential requires believing in ourselves and being confident in who we are.
Our potential will not grow or be realised unless we choose to put action to it.

What do you believe about yourself?

"Your potential is really up to you. It doesn't matter what others might think. It doesn't matter where you came from. It doesn't even matter what you might have believed about yourself at a previous time in your life. It's about what lies within you and whether you can bring it out."[4]

JOHN C. MAXWELL

[4] Maxwell. J., (2007) *Talent is Never Enough.* (pg 18) Tennessee: Thomas Nelson.

laying the foundation.
GROUP DISCUSSION: SEEDS OF GREATNESS

Hold up a tiny apple seed for the group to see. This seed has the potential to be an orchard. A seed produces an apple tree, which produces apples which produce more seeds. These seeds produce more apple trees, apples and seeds. The growth is ongoing. Seeds have so much potential. Our purpose cannot grow unless we first recognise we have seeds of potential within us.

'Everything that we need to live the life we want is already planted inside us.'

Q. How do we look after our seeds of greatness?
- We nurture the seeds by valuing ourselves.
- Create the right environment to bring forth the life we want – surround ourselves with healthy relationships, positive role models, and encouraging people.
- Being positive and believing in our potential.
- Give ourselves opportunity to develop and try new things.
- Keep our health in balance – physically, emotionally, mentally, spiritually.

We can live our life as a garden. What grows is what we plant and what we let others plant in it. We can choose what seeds we plant in our own garden. Seeds can be skills, knowledge, experiences, thoughts and ideas.

presentation.
ACTIVITY: PLANTING A SEED

Ask the women to write their names on their cup. Then place a little bit of potting mix inside, plant the seed, add more potting mix and then water.

Each woman has their planted seed in front of them. Even though they can't see the seed, it is planted inside their cup. Often in life, if we can't see our potential, we consequently overlook it – 'There is no seed in here', 'I have no potential.' Just because we can't see the seed doesn't mean it isn't within us and it isn't growing. We need to believe in our potential!

Provide examples of people who lived in their potential.

ACTIVITY: CHOOSING CONFIDENCE.

CONFIDENCE | kon-fi-d*uh* ns l |
Full trust: belief in the trustworthiness or reliability of a person or thing, boldness, self-assurance and poise.

Confidence comes from embracing who we are. To live in our potential sometimes requires us to step out of our comfort zone and do new things. How confident we grow is our choice. A key to living in our potential is choosing to believe in ourselves and be confident. To get something we don't have, sometimes we need to do something we haven't done before.

Q. Where is our confidence found? Are we born with it?
Q. What are some things that can hinder you from growing in your potential?
Q. Is there something standing in your way of moving toward growing the seed that is within you?
Q. Have you failed in an area and have given up on that seed?

Write that obstacle on a piece of paper. Now close your eyes and think about achieving your potential and envision yourself moving toward growing that seed. Don't allow any negative thoughts to come in and distract you from achieving that potential. After you have seen yourself reaching your potential and nurturing that seed of greatness, take that piece of paper, crumple it up and walk confidently down the walkway and throw it in the bin.

You can even have the women declare 'My potential is limitless!' at the end.

discussion and wrap-up.
Q. What can you do with these seeds starting today?

ASSESS OUTCOMES
Reinforce Purpose concept. Affirm the group as a whole or to each individual by name 'My potential is limitless'. This exercise is a powerful way to end a session.

shine factor.
IDEAS: A bag of seeds, juicy apple, 'seeds of greatness' quote (see Appendix F).

note to facilitator.
This can be a very powerful exercise. Keep the atmosphere light-hearted and fun. Ensure you have some good music. Look out for women who may need extra care and encouragement.

'I HAVE A HOPE AND A FUTURE'

purpose.

SESSION EIGHT MY LIFE HAS PURPOSE

MATERIAL REQUIRED: Cardboard – 1 A4/A3 sheet per person, glue, gel pens/pastels/permanent markers, scissors, stickers, sticky tape, magazines or pre-cut magazine clippings, newspapers, name badges, whiteboard and whiteboard markers, IMAGINE handout (see Appendix G).

Please see recommended layout below.

ACTIVITY	DETAILS	NOTES/MATERIALS
Icebreaker (15 mins)	Activity: Wrap up a gift	RESOURCES: Wrapping material
Power Focus (5 mins)	'MY LIFE HAS PURPOSE'	
Laying The Foundation (10 mins)	Q. What is your heart song? Q. What is your life's blueprint?	
Presentation (50 mins)	ACTIVITIES: Talents Vision Dream Collage	RESOURCES: Paper, pens, glue, collage materials, newspaper, sticky tape, IMAGINE handout.
Group Discussion and Wrap-up (10 mins)	Q. How can I live my dreams? Q. How can I make a positive contribution to others? Reinforce Purpose concept 'MY LIFE HAS PURPOSE'	
Shine Factor	As you give out the gifts, encourage each woman	Gifts

outcomes.
By the end of this session, each woman will be able to:
IDENTIFY PERSONAL DESIRES AND STRENGTHS
DEVELOP AN UNDERSTANDING THAT SHE HAS SOMETHING TO CONTRIBUTE

icebreaker.

ACTIVITY: WRAP UP A GIFT

Have each woman wrap a small gift with 'love' for someone else. Give them resources to wrap and decorate the gift. Provide different coloured wrapping paper, ribbons and so forth. Try to be as creative as possible with wrapping up the gift (which could be nail polish, an apple, a chocolate bar or basically anything new). As the gift is for someone else, encourage them to make the gift special.

PURPOSE: 'Our life is a gift'. Our life is designed to be a gift to others. Our smile, our love, our care and kind words are a gift to people around us. We are valuable. This gives us a new spin on life. Living is not just about getting through the day-to-day activities; it is also about those moments that fill our heart with joy and gladness. We can contribute to the world around us.

The point of this activity is not about what they are wrapping up, but about understanding that their life is a gift. For alternative icebreakers see Appendix A.

power focus.
'MY LIFE HAS PURPOSE.'

We are unique; there is no one else like us. How we are designed, our passions, our talents, and our strengths are unique to each of us and have purpose. All these qualities are in us so that we can fulfil our personal desires. There is a blueprint inside all of us. We are purpose-built and exist for a reason. There is a purpose for our life.

Discovering our purpose is a key aspect to every person's journey. We get a taste of our purpose when we tap into the desires of our heart. What satisfies us and what makes us frustrated? We each have a specific wiring with a palette of gifts and strengths that are as unique to each individual as a thumbprint!

Developing our gifts and talents, identifying our dreams and desires and learning how to use them, all help us to live a life of purpose. Purpose enables us to make a difference in our world. Life does not have to be about just living for ourselves. Our life can be used to make a difference for others.

We can choose to live in a world that is about ourselves or we can choose to include others in our world and make a difference.

laying the foundation.

Q. What is your heart's song?

The world we live in can try to label us, put titles on us and make us try and fit into a certain box, telling us 'This is the way to be significant, popular or successful'.

In the movie Happy Feet, young Mumble's song was not singing, but tap dancing. This is what he was born to do, yet his behaviour was 'un-penguin' like. We all have a song to sing. We all have a message over our life, a reason for our existence, and a purpose to our life.

What melody does your heart sing? What flows naturally from your life?

By being true to ourselves, we can find our heart song and use it to create a difference in the world. In turn, others have the choice to do the same. Suggest the women watch the movie Happy Feet as an example of a heart song on their own time.

presentation.

ACTIVITY: VISION

Q. Have you ever imagined yourself accomplishing your dreams?
Q. Do you keep that vision of victory in front of you?
Q. Do you most often see yourself winning or losing, succeeding or failing?

Write down any dreams that you haven't been able to imagine yourself fulfilling. This can involve writing a vision statement for your life.

ACTIVITY: TALENTS

Split the group up into small groups. Give each group lots of newspapers and sticky tape and get them to create something out of it. An example could be to make something really tall, or make an object or building such as the Eiffel Tower, or the Sydney Harbour Bridge. As the facilitator, watch the different roles the women take up.

After the groups have finished creating, from observation explain the different roles that the women performed. There is the visionary, the project manager, the do-er, and the facilitator. Encourage a group discussion on this. What did the women observe about themselves and others?

TALENT | tal-*uh* nt |

A special natural ability, qualities; a capacity for achievement or success; ability; a person who possesses unusual innate ability in some field or activity.

We have each been wonderfully made. Spend some time thinking about and celebrating your strengths, talents and abilities. What we are good at can be used to help others.

Ways to identify talents. Ask yourself:
- What am I good at or what do people say I am good at?
- What do I love doing?
- What comes naturally to me?

'Everyone has strengths and talents.'

"When you find purpose, you find passion. And when you find passion, it energises your talent so that you can achieve excellence."[5]

JOHN C. MAXWELL

5   Maxwell, J., (2007) *Talent is Never Enough*. (pg 40) Tennessee: Thomas Nelson.

ACTIVITY: DREAM COLLAGE

This activity is about each woman creatively expressing their dreams and desires for their future through creating a 'dream' collage. This activity is significant, as it gives women the opportunity to dream big for their future. A visual representation of one's hopes and dreams is a powerful message that can inspire, strengthen and encourage us in our personal journey of purpose and significance. The activity is also a great technique for women to begin their discovery of how unique they are.

Write on the board:

If money, time, place, ability, education and confidence were not an issue, what would you do with your life? (If you knew you could not fail, what would you do?)

Hand out the IMAGINE handout (see Appendix G) to the group and use this to discuss the focus of understanding 'My life has purpose'. Distribute to each woman a piece of cardboard and ask them to write their name in the centre. Distribute magazines, scissors, glue and pens. Show the women an example collage.

Give the participants license to dream, imagine, reflect and create what they desire. Encourage the women to imagine the paper as a blank canvas.

Words and images both contribute to a strong statement about their life dreams. Laminate collages once completed if the women desire.

When they are finished, ask a few of the women (all women if time permits) to present their collage to the rest of the group. Encourage them to find a special place for it where they can see it and be inspired to go for it!

Explore 'IMAGINE' handout before attempting the dream collage.

IMAGINE

BIRTHDAY SPEECHES

Imagine it is your birthday. What would you like people to say about you for your birthday speech? What would you like people to write about you on your birthday card?

LIKES

If you had the total approval and admiration of everyone, regardless of what you do, what would you do with your life?

ROLE MODELS

What role models do you look up to? Who inspires you? What personal strengths or qualities do they have that you admire?

CHARACTER STRENGTHS

What personal strengths and qualities do you already have? Which ones would you like to develop? How would you like to apply them?

WEALTH

Imagine you win the lottery or inherit a fortune. How would you spend it? Who would you share it with?

watch out for
DREAM STEALERS!

FEAR

SELF-DOUBT

NEGATIVE COMMENTS

CHALLENGING CIRCUMSTANCES

LACK OF CONFIDENCE

LACK OF MOTIVATION
Too busy to focus on yourself and what makes you happy.

LACK OF SELF-VALUE
Believing other things are more important than you.

PRINCIPLES FOR LIVING YOUR POTENTIAL:
- Believe you are able
- Believe it is possible *YES – GOAL – ACTION PLAN*
- Pay the price/work hard
- Don't get discouraged by failure
- Be confident. Confidence brings great reward.

small group discussion.

Q. What can I do now to live my dreams?
Q. Who do I have in my life that I can share my dreams with and keep me accountable?
Q. How can I make a positive contribution to others?

A suggestion is to have the participants join with one another and plan to give a special experience to someone else outside the group or give their time to someone in need. Encourage them to do what comes to them no matter how 'out of the comfort zone' it might be. Encourage them to take the time now to plan their adventure in value.

GIVE EXAMPLES: someone they know, local nursing home, partnering with a not-for-profit organization such as World Vision, or doing acts of kindness for the homeless. Commit to each other who/where/when and do it during this coming week if possible.

ASSESS OUTCOMES
Reinforce Purpose concept. Affirm the group as a whole or to each individual by name 'My life has purpose.' This exercise is a powerful way to end a session.

shine factor.
IDEAS: Dream collage, pen (to write history with), Martin Luther King Jr. quote.

If you did the 'wrap up a gift' activity, get each woman to take their gift and turn to the person next to them. They are to exchange gifts. Encourage them to offer encouragement to the other person, and speak from their heart with love as they present their gift. Make sure they take turns – not simultaneously!!

note to facilitator.
This is a big session with a lot to fit in, and every part is important. Be well prepared and keep it to the timeframe. Be aware that some women may not be aware of any hopes or dreams for their future.

'I HAVE A HOPE AND A FUTURE'

9
purpose.
SESSION NINE SHINE!

MATERIAL REQUIRED: Feedback forms, Tea Cup Story handout, Graduation certificates, food and refreshments, whiteboard markers, whiteboard, Celebrating the Shine Journey handout (see Appendix I)

Please see recommended layout below.

ACTIVITY	DETAILS	NOTES/MATERIALS
Icebreaker (10 mins)	Activity: Personal testimonies	
Presentation (60 mins)	OPTIONS: 1. Movie night 2. Special outing 3. Pass the 'ShineWOMEN' message on to others	
Celebration and Presentation of Certificates (15 mins)	Present certificates to graduates	RESOURCES: Graduation certificates.
Shine Factor	As you give out the gifts, encourage each woman	Gifts

outcomes.
By the end of this session, each woman will be able to:
DESCRIBE WHAT SHE HAS LEARNT

icebreaker.
ACTIVITY: PERSONAL STORIES
Ask the women to share what they think their purpose may be or encourage the women to share what they have learnt from ShineWOMEN.

presentation.
HERE ARE 3 OPTIONS TO CHOOSE BETWEEN:
1. Plan in advance an outing to a swish hotel or restaurant to treat the women to a special time. This could be coffee and dessert, a light supper or whatever you are able to do. Maybe you can create a special room with a WOW factor for the women. Whatever it is, it'll be a great surprise for the women. Transport needs to be arranged. Bus/cars – keep it smooth and ensure every part of the experience makes the women feel special

2. Hold a movie night at a special location. It could be at someone's home or another function room. Choose a movie that is uplifting and inspirational. Create the atmosphere with candles, cushions and throw rugs. Design a menu with a choice of beverages and light snacks (see Appendix H for a sample). Suggested movies that relate to living life with purpose: One Night with The King – The story of Queen Esther and her life's purpose, Ghandi, Mother Teresa, Amazing Grace, Forrest Gump, Coach Carter, Freedom Writers

3. Pass the ShineWOMEN message on to others Explore and discuss with the group what they have learnt from ShineWOMEN and what ways they can pass on what they have learnt to others. Some suggestions include:
   - Write (and make) an encouragement card.
   - Spend quality time with someone in need.
   - Write a thank you card to someone in a nursing home for their life and contribution they have made to society.

celebration and presentation of certificates.

At this time all the ladies will be seated. This celebration gives the opportunity for each woman to stand up, receive her certificate and declare statements about herself. There is power in speaking aloud.

Q. What do you stand for or what kind of declaration would you like to make over your life?

- I am valuable
- I am one-of-a-kind
- I am wonderfully made
- I have the power of choice
- My decisions determine my destination
- I have resilience
- My potential is limitless
- My life has purpose

ASSESS OUTCOMES
Encourage women to stay connected and build on the networks they have made during the group if possible.

shine factor.
IDEAS: The Shine scroll handout rolled up and tied with ribbon. See Appendix I.

note to facilitator.
See Appendix I for an example of a certificate.

A
appendices.

SHINEWOMEN MATERIALS

A. ALTERNATIVE ICEBREAKERS
B. I AM VALUABLE
C. I AM WONDERFULLY MADE
D. I HAVE THE POWER OF CHOICE
E. MY DECISIONS DETERMINE MY DESTINATION
F. MY POTENTIAL IS LIMITLESS - SEEDS OF GREATNESS QUOTE
G. MY LIFE HAS PURPOSE
H. CELEBRATION SAMPLE MENU
I. SHINE SCROLL AND CERTIFICATE
J. A TEACUP STORY

APPENDIX A - ALTERNATIVE ICEBREAKERS

Icebreakers are fun and interactive. Icebreakers appeal to all 3 key learning styles – learning by seeing, learning by experiencing for oneself and learning by hearing. Participants immediately feel involved and part of the group. This allows the group to feel relaxed and begin to bond. Remember: don't force anyone to participate! The following are examples only. Feel free to be creative and adapt activities to best fit your group.

ACTIVITY: TRUTH OR FALSE

Everything that has happened to us, every experience and every word spoken over us can affect the way we think about who we are. Through these experiences we form beliefs about ourselves, others and about life.

With the group, discuss any self-doubt thoughts they may have. List them on the whiteboard under two columns; one labelled 'False' and the other labelled 'Truth'. Each thought that is not truth, place under the 'False' column. Once the column has been filled discuss with the group what the truth might be to each 'False' thought that is written down. Place these in the 'Truth' column.

Encourage the team to initiate suggestions. If the women feel anything stands out for them personally, encourage them to write it down. Examples are:

False	*Truth*
I am incapable.	I am more than capable.
I am useless.	I am of use for good.
I am stupid.	I am smart.
I have no voice.	My opinion counts for much.
I have no control.	I can choose for myself.
I am ugly.	I am unique and beautiful.
I talk too much.	What I have to say matters.
I am unlovable.	I am loved.
I am a burden.	I am helpful.
I can't do anything right.	I can do things right.

Using 3 x 5 index cards have the women write down something they would like to challenge about what they believe about themselves (what women speak over their lives is usually a good start). Now, challenge the women to honestly question this belief and if it is not true have them write 'This is false' underneath the belief. Example:

Now turn the card over and write the truth

i am worthless.	i am wonderfully made.
This is false	**This is truth**

BENEFITS: Communication skills, changing negative mindsets, group bonding and comfort zones.

APPENDIX A - ALTERNATIVE ICEBREAKERS

IF I WERE A PAINTER
Finish the sentence 'If I were a painter, I would paint a picture of...?'

BENEFITS: Communication skills, team building, aids self-awareness

GIFT EXCHANGE
Using your Shine Factor for the day, set out the table with enough gifts for everyone (this works best if it's the same gift). Have sufficient wrapping paper/tissue paper, scissors and tape for the group to wrap one item each. Add ribbon and anything else creative like stickers, flowers and so forth. Display first to the group 'How To' wrap a gift and then add ribbon and a touch of creativity to inspire theirs. Curling ribbon or adding two colours together can be fun.

BENEFITS: Self-awareness (what I like), team building, creativity, relaxing, fun!

GETTING TO KNOW YOU
This exercise is great to use when you are aware of the dynamics of your group and that they like to chat, as it encourages open sharing. Give permission for anyone to pass. Ask each person to share something that they have learnt since the group had started. What have they gleaned or what has inspired them? Or simply recap what we did last week!

BENEFITS: Opens communication, self-awareness, group bonding, peer awareness.

FINISH THIS SENTENCE
Using sentence completion allows each person to share something about them in a 'safe' way. Make this fun and on the light side, not too serious. These can be put on a handout or on a whiteboard/poster. If I could do anything I would like to…If I were to write a book it would be…If I were a musical instrument I would be…My favourite movie of all time is…What makes me laugh is…

BENEFITS: Opens communication, self-awareness, group bonding!

GREETINGS
Provide either blank cards or have the group create a card with an envelope. Ask the group to think of someone they would like to give the card to and write something special on the inside. Provide stamps if needed.

BENEFITS: Communication, creativity, promotes generosity.

TWO TRUTHS AND A LIE
Each person tells three things about themselves; two true and one not true. The group tries to guess which is not true.

BENEFITS: Communication, Fun!

APPENDIX A - ALTERNATIVE ICEBREAKERS

IF I WERE A PAINTER
Finish the sentence 'If I were a painter, I would paint a picture of...?'

BENEFITS: Communication skills, team building, aids self-awareness

GIFT EXCHANGE
Using your Shine Factor for the day, set out the table with enough gifts for everyone (this works best if it's the same gift). Have sufficient wrapping paper/tissue paper, scissors and tape for the group to wrap one item each. Add ribbon and anything else creative like stickers, flowers and so forth. Display first to the group 'How To' wrap a gift and then add ribbon and a touch of creativity to inspire theirs. Curling ribbon or adding two colours together can be fun.

BENEFITS: Self-awareness (what I like), team building, creativity, relaxing, fun!

GETTING TO KNOW YOU
This exercise is great to use when you are aware of the dynamics of your group and that they like to chat, as it encourages open sharing. Give permission for anyone to pass. Ask each person to share something that they have learnt since the group had started. What have they gleaned or what has inspired them? Or simply recap what we did last week!

interesting facts about.
HANDS.

each hand contains...
- 29 major and minor bones.
- At least 123 named ligaments.
- 34 muscles that move the fingers and thumb.
- 48 nerves and 30 named arteries.
- A quarter of the part of the brain that controls movement in the body is devoted to the muscles of the hands.
- There are no muscles in your fingers. The muscles that move your fingers are located in the palm and up in the forearm.
- Your fingernails grow about the same amount as the continents move every year.
- It takes 6 months for your fingernails to grow all the way from the root to tip, and structurally, fingernails are modified hairs.
- Everyone has unique patterns on their palms and fingertips. The palm of your hands and the soles of your feet have the thickest skin of the human body.
- Our palms are hairless and don't tan. While being tough and durable, our hands are very sensitive.

hands are expressive and creative.
- They touch: one of the 5 senses
- They massage, stroke, caress
- They speak emotion: happiness, anger, nervousness, excitement.
- They grasp and embrace
- They pull and push
- They guide and point
- They can tell a story: weathered, tanned, rough, calloused, manicured, wrinkled, soft, dry.

hands in action.
- A handshake
- A helping hand
- A soothing hand
- A hand up and a hand out
- A hand of friendship
- A hand extends to the poor and to the needy
- Creation: they make/cook and creativity: music/art, etc
- They bring gifts to people.

The single most important thing we can do to keep from getting sick and spreading illness is to clean our hands. Think about touching tables, doorknobs, desks and telephones; bacteria from hands can survive from 20 mins – 2 hrs (and some strains even longer).

NAIL CARE.

At the beginning of the session discuss the importance of looking after our hands to prevent minor nail damage, splits and tears. We value ourselves by preventing damage. Divide the class into groups of four and hand out the nail care items. Encourage the women to care for each other's nails: filing, buffing, painting. Talk to the participants about how to file, buff and paint, including benefits. Nail cutting is not permitted.

Activity: Mini manicure

Teach the women how to do an 8-step manicure.

Manicure material: Nail polish remover, buffers, nail files, nail polish, hand cream, manicure handout.
The topics to cover are: The need and advantages of nail care, steps involved to do a manicure, nail damage – splits, tears, biting, choosing a nail polish colour, maintaining nails and hands.

WHY CARE?
Regular and attentive care is necessary if you want healthy nails. It is essential as fingernails deteriorate very quickly if neglected. The actual manicure procedure helps the nail grow in the correct way, freeing the cuticle (skin around the base of the nail) and nail wall from the nail plate. Regular attention will also prevent minor nail damage, splits and tears. The outline of the nail is kept smooth, infection is prevented and only gentle treatment is required to maintain an attractive set of nails.

TO MANICURE

1. Remove old polish. For natural nails, use an acetone-free remover.
2. Apply cuticle oil on the cuticles and rub in.
3. File nails to desired shape. File your nails in one direction, starting at the edges and moving toward the top. Use clippers to trim any split or ragged tips. To make your nails look more even, trim your longest nails until they are about the same length as their shorter counterparts.
4. Soak in warm water for a few minutes to soften cuticles.
5. Tidy up cuticles (cuticles are the skin that overlaps onto the nails). Use a cuticle stick to push back cuticles. Be sure not to cut your cuticles, which can cause infection and damage the nails.
6. Wipe nails with a damp cloth to remove excess oils.
7. Apply a base coat (ensure hands are clean and free from any residual oil).
8. Apply a clear coat or your favourite colour. Always apply polish by starting on the side of the nail. You should be able to cover the nail in three strokes, one on each side and one in the middle. Let it dry!

Correct potential mess-ups. Roll a small amount of cotton to a cuticle stick and apply the remover around the nail.

BUFFING

1. Buffing is an alternative to polishing your nails during a home manicure session.
2. Swipe the rough side of the buff against each nail to smooth away the ridges and discolouration.
3. Use the other side to smooth and shine the nails.
4. Buffing can leave you with smooth and healthy looking nails.
5. Ensure that you sanitise your home manicure products and equipment before you dry and store them away.

NAIL CARE HINTS

1. To make nail polish dry quicker, put the bottle in the freezer for a few minutes before you use it, or rinse your hands after you remove old polish; the water washes away chemical residue and oils, which slows the drying time.
2. Wear gloves in cold weather and when cleaning or washing up.
3. Treat cuticles gently, to avoid ridging or white spots appearing on your nails. A degree of ridging on the nail is natural for some people. Eat protein and calcium-rich foods. Illness, nervous stress and poor diet can be detrimental to strong, healthy nails.
4. White spots on the fingernail may indicate a vitamin B deficiency.
5. Gently file nails with smooth, even strokes. File one way only – from side to centre. Only file nails when dry and firm. If you must cut them, do it after a bath or shower, when they are soft and pliable. If long nails need to be greatly shortened, clip them before filing.

HAIR CARE.

A GREAT WAY TO SHAMPOO
Shampooing is the first step in hair care, and is important if you want to achieve healthy looking hair.

GET THE MOST OUT OF YOUR SHAMPOO
1. Pour a small amount of shampoo into palms; rub together for a thick lather.
2. Massage shampoo gently into hair working downward from forehead, concentrating on hairline around the ears, working towards the back of the neck.
3. Rinse thoroughly (water should be lukewarm for dry hair and cool for oily hair to help close pores).

A GREAT WAY TO CONDITION
Now that you're on your way to healthy looking hair, finish with a conditioner designed for your hair type. Conditioning helps restore vitality to hair damaged by the stress of the sun, wind, pollution, electric hair appliances, and other factors such as dieting, smoking and illness. Conditioners need to be combed through before being rinsed out thoroughly.

MY STYLE
A great haircut is basic to any hairstyle. It may be one length or layered. Many times the haircut is the style itself. The key to a great hairstyle is regular cutting – every 6 to 8 weeks.

HAIR CARE HINTS
1. Avoid combs with sharp teeth or rough edges that can irritate the scalp and break hair. Avoid harsh nylon or metal bristle brushes.
2. Avoid using rubber bands in your hair; always use coated elastic when you wear your hair back and never put your hair back too tightly.
3. To help protect your hair from the harmful effect of chlorine or salt water, apply hair moisturiser to damp hair after a day at the beach
4. Leave for one hour and rinse out.
5. Massaging egg yolk and olive oil into your hair is a good hair reviver – don't forget to rinse it out well!
6. Take extra care if you have a colour in your hair. Chlorine and salt water can discolour your hair.

APPENDIX D - I HAVE THE POWER OF CHOICE

STRENGTH IS...

BUILDING ON GOOD RELATIONSHIPS

CHOOSING TO MAKE OUR EXPERIENCES COUNT

LOOKING FOR THE GOOD IN ALL THINGS

ASKING FOR HELP WHEN WE NEED IT

HAVING AN ATTITUDE OF GRATITUDE

RESPONDING AND NOT REACTING TO OUR SITUATION

LIVING A LIFE TRUE TO OUR VALUES AND CONVICTIONS

ALLOWING OTHERS TO COME ALONGSIDE TO SUPPORT US

BELIEVING THE TRUTH ABOUT OURSELVES

HAVING HEALTHY BOUNDARIES AND RESPECT

APPENDIX D - I HAVE THE POWER OF CHOICE

STOP.
THINK.
CH●●SE.

We decide how we want to behave. Don't let your **FEELINGS** *decide for you but take your feelings into* **CONSIDERATION** *and use them to your* **ADVANTAGE.**

STOP.
THINK.
CH●●SE.

We decide how we want to behave. Don't let your **FEELINGS** *decide for you but take your feelings into* **CONSIDERATION** *and use them to your* **ADVANTAGE.**

STOP.
THINK.
CH●●SE.

We decide how we want to behave. Don't let your **FEELINGS** *decide for you but take your feelings into* **CONSIDERATION** *and use them to your* **ADVANTAGE.**

STOP.
THINK.
CH●●SE.

We decide how we want to behave. Don't let your **FEELINGS** *decide for you but take your feelings into* **CONSIDERATION** *and use them to your* **ADVANTAGE.**

APPENDIX D - I HAVE THE POWER OF CHOICE

ANGRY

HAPPY

SAD

FEARFUL

COMBINATION

APPENDIX D - I HAVE THE POWER OF CHOICE

FURIOUS

IRRITATED

ANNOYED

TICKED OFF

HUMILIATED

APPENDIX D - I HAVE THE POWER OF CHOICE

FRUSTRATED

HURT

SARCASTIC

DISGUSTED

APPENDIX D - I HAVE THE POWER OF CHOICE

EXCITED

SATISFIED

PLEASED

JOYFUL

DELIGHTED

APPENDIX D - I HAVE THE POWER OF CHOICE

COMFORTABLE

HOPEFUL

SURPRISED

POSITIVE

APPENDIX D - I HAVE THE POWER OF CHOICE

GRIEF

MISERABLE

DOWN

DISAPPOINTED

HURT

LONELY

FORGOTTEN

REMORSEFUL

REJECTED

APPENDIX D - I HAVE THE POWER OF CHOICE

NERVOUS

TERRIFIED

ANXIOUS

WORRIED

CONCERNED

APPENDIX D - I HAVE THE POWER OF CHOICE

AFRAID

UNCERTAIN

OUT OF CONTROL

UNEASY

APPENDIX D - I HAVE THE POWER OF CHOICE

GUILTY

JEALOUS

SHAME

EMBARRASSED

UNCOMFORTABLE

CONFUSED

TORN

ENVIOUS

COMPASSION

APPENDIX E - MY DECISIONS DETERMINE MY DESTINATION

STRENGTH
the Journey of a Diamond

Natural Process – HEAT & PRESSURE

Diamonds begin as rocks that are deep below the earth's surface. Under conditions of extreme heat and pressure these rocks form diamonds.

These same conditions force the diamond to the surface for the earth.

FACT Diamonds are the strongest substance on earth!

Diamonds can only be produced by the earth, but its brilliance can only be produced by the refining of man.

Man Process – DISCOVERY & REFINING PROCESS

Uncut diamonds cannot reflect their true beauty.

A diamond can only be cut and polished by other diamonds – by rubbing against each other.

The diamonds are first cut in their weak areas to remove impurities and irregularities.

FACT Diamonds without flaws are extremely rare.

FACT No diamond is exactly the same.

The effort put into the refining process determines the brilliance of the diamond.
You are the BEST!

APPENDIX F - MY POTENTIAL IS LIMITLESS - SEEDS OF GREATNESS QUOTE

Seeds of Greatness
"I believe the seeds of greatness are within us all. The key is in creating the correct environment for them to then surface into reality"

Seeds of Greatness
"I believe the seeds of greatness are within us all. The key is in creating the correct environment for them to then surface into reality"

Seeds of Greatness
"I believe the seeds of greatness are within us all. The key is in creating the correct environment for them to then surface into reality"

Seeds of Greatness
"I believe the seeds of greatness are within us all. The key is in creating the correct environment for them to then surface into reality"

Seeds of Greatness
"I believe the seeds of greatness are within us all. The key is in creating the correct environment for them to then surface into reality"

Seeds of Greatness
"I believe the seeds of greatness are within us all. The key is in creating the correct environment for them to then surface into reality"

APPENDIX G - MY LIFE HAS PURPOSE

IMAGINE

BIRTHDAY SPEECHES

Imagine it is your birthday. What would you like people to say about you for your birthday speech? What would you like people to write about you on your birthday card?

LIKES

If you had the total approval and admiration of everyone, regardless of what you do, what would you do with your life?

ROLE MODELS

What role models do you look up to? Who inspires you? What personal strengths or qualities do they have that you admire?

CHARACTER STRENGTHS

What personal strengths and qualities do you already have? Which ones would you like to develop? How would you like to apply them?

WEALTH

Imagine you win the lottery or inherit a fortune. How would you spend it? Who would you share it with?

APPENDIX H - CELEBRATION SAMPLE MENU

PLEASE TICK YOUR SELECTION

desserts

☐ **BON VIVANT (WHEAT FREE)**

The Bon Vivant is a signature creation consisting of two layers; the first a soft flourless hazelnut cake, the top a smooth baked chocolate mousse.

Scrumptious!

☐ **ORANGE ALMOND TORTE (WHEAT & DAIRY FREE)**

A flourless cake, made with oranges and almond meal.
Finished with an apricot glaze and a border of flaked almonds.

Delicious...

☐ **BLUEBERRY CHEESECAKE**

Speaks for itself... *Mmmmm...*

drinks

☐ coffee   ☐ tea   ☐ herbal tea   ☐ hot chocolate

EXTRAS

☐ full cream milk   ☐ skim milk   ☐ no milk   ☐ sugar ___ tsp

APPENDIX I - SHINE SCROLL AND CERTIFICATE

THIS IS TO CERTIFY THAT...

i have and will always have...

WORTH!

BODY AND SOUL, I AM WONDERFULLY MADE! I AM SOMEBODY!! I HAVE IMMEASURABLE VALUE.

I am unique, matchless and incomparable; no one in the *ENTIRE* world at present or in *ALL* the ages of time has my great gifts, abilities, heart or talents. What a woman I AM... no one has been me and no one will *EVER* be like me. Because *I AM WORTH TAKING CARE OF MYSELF*, I remind myself and the world that *"I AM A MASTERPIECE!"* There is nobody like me and there will never be anyone like me. I can't fit into anybody else's mould. I can't be compared to anyone... not even my sister, mother or friends. My *WORTH* is not related to my performance and what I do – but to my very being. My *WORTH* cannot be earned. It is inborn. I was born with this immeasurable value!!

i have and will always have...

STRENGTH!

My strength comes when I use my self-control for good, for myself and for others.
Choosing safe friends, good decision-making (with my mind & not from my feelings) which empowers me to *ACT* and not *REACT*. The quality of my life is a direct result of *MY* choices. Stop. Think. Choose.

i have and will always have...

PURPOSE!

MY LIFE COUNTS. I AM UNIQUE! I HAVE PURPOSE.
I am custom made, a masterpiece, one-of-a-kind. I will be the best ME that I can be.
I have to realise that if I'm going to succeed; failing can be a part of the journey...
the important part to remember is to not stay down!

Never a failure, always a lesson.

I will learn from my mistakes and move forward.
It doesn't matter where I've been; It's where I'm going that counts!
I am able to rise above any circumstance and turn it into good!

SHINE FACILITATOR   SHINE CO-FACILITATOR   DATE

CERTIFICATE OF **ACHIEVEMENT** TO RECOGNISE

FOR SUCCESSFULLY COMPLETING **SHINEWOMEN**

"i will be the best me that i can be!"

APPENDIX J - A TEACUP STORY

A couple went into an antique shop one day and found a beautiful teacup sitting on a shelf. They took it off the shelf, so they could look at it more closely, and said, "We really want to buy this gorgeous cup."

All of the sudden, the teacup began to talk, saying, "I wasn't always like this. There was a time when I was just a cold, hard, colourless lump of clay. One day my master picked me up and said, 'I could do something with this.' Then he started to pat me, and roll me, and change my shape."

"I said, 'What are you doing? That hurts. I don't know if I want to look like this! Stop!' But he said, 'Not yet.'"

"Then he put me on a wheel and began to spin me around and around and around, until I screamed, 'Let me off, I am getting dizzy!' 'Not yet,' he said.

"Then he shaped me into a cup and put me in a hot oven. I cried, 'Let me out! It's hot in here, I am suffocating.' But he just looked at me through that little glass window and smiled and said, 'Not yet.'"

"When he took me out, I thought his work on me was over, but then he started to paint me. I couldn't believe what he did next. He put me back into the oven, and I said, 'You have to believe me, I can't stand this! Please let me out!' But he said, 'Not yet.'"

"Finally, he took me out of the oven and set me up on a shelf where I thought he had forgotten me. Then one day he took me off the shelf and held me before a mirror. I couldn't believe my eyes, I had become a beautiful teacup that everyone wants to buy."

AUTHOR UNKNOWN

NOTES

NOTES

NOTES

NOTES

NOTES

NOTES

NOTES

NOTES

NOTES

NOTES

NOTES

NOTES

NOTES

NOTES

NOTES

NOTES

NOTES

NOTES

NOTES

NOTES

NOTES

NOTES

NOTES

NOTES

NOTES

www.ingramcontent.com/pod-product-compliance
Lightning Source LLC
Chambersburg PA
CBHW080809300426
44114CB00020B/2876